The Witches' Almanac

Spring 2010 — Spring 2011

CONTAINING pictorial and explicit delineations of the
magical phases of the Moon together with information about astrological
portents of the year to come and various aspects of occult knowledge
enabling all who read to improve their lives in the old manner.

The Witches' Almanac, Ltd.

Publishers   Providence, Rhode Island
www.TheWitchesAlmanac.com

Address all inquiries and information to
THE WITCHES' ALMANAC, LTD.
P.O. Box 1292
Newport, RI 02840-9998

10-ISBN: 0-9773703-7-2
13-ISBN: 978-0-9773703-7-5

ISSN: 1522-3183

First Printing August 2009

Printed in Canada

Printed on 100% recycled paper

Established 1971 by Elizabeth Pepper

Preface

ANIMALS ARE OUR FRIENDS, companions, healers, spell-workers and for the witches among us, our familiars.

From feral to domestic creatures, we sense connection on some level. We see to it that our animal companions are well cared for, well fed and petted to a loving degree – as my dear friend Hans Holzer used to say, "that is why they are called pets." We form a symbiotic relationship with our pets – mutually considerate for and learning from the other. The fundamental bond between a witch and a familiar is of the utmost importance – for each, bringing emotional and spiritual strength and support.

We know that domesticated animals cannot survive the wilderness. These are two different worlds, separated by a backyard fence, wall or hedge. In addition to marking the boundary between the "civilized" and the "wild," these borders represent the subtle veil between the conscious and the unconscious, or the world of the living and the realm of the mighty dead. Unlike ourselves, our familiars are, in some way, a part of both worlds. Although domesticated, they are more suited to survive in the wild than humans are. Animals are in closer contact with their instincts, humans more prone to rational thought.

A true familiar is one with the witch – sharing the same nourishment, suffering the same pains. The more time you spend with your companion, the closer the bond becomes, making the communication easier and your magic stronger. This advantage can be shared both in this world and the next. Appreciate familiars for what they are – a loving extension of ourselves.

❧ HOLIDAYS ❧

Spring 2010 to Spring 2011

Art Director . . . . Karen Marks
Astrologer . . . . Dikki-Jo Mullen
Climatologist . . . . Tom C. Lang
Cover Art and Design. . . Ogmios MacMerlin
Production Consultant . . . . Robin Antoni
Sales . . . . Ellen Lynch
Shipping, Bookkeeping . . . . D. Bullock

ANDREW THEITIC
Executive Editor

❧

BARBARA STACY
JEAN MARIE WALSH
Associate Editors

CONTENTS

The Tyger

TYGER, tyger, burning bright
In the forests of the night,
What immortal hand or eye
Could frame thy fearful symmetry?

In what distant deeps or skies
Burnt the fire of thine eyes?
On what wings dare he aspire?
What the hand dare seize the fire?

And what shoulder and what art
Could twist the sinews of thy heart?
And when thy heart began to beat,
What dread hand and what dread feet?

What the hammer? what the chain?
In what furnace was thy brain?
What the anvil? What dread grasp
Dare its deadly terrors clasp?

When the stars threw down their spears,
And water'd heaven with their tears,
Did he smile his work to see?
Did he who made the Lamb make thee?

Tyger, tyger, burning bright
In the forests of the night,
What immortal hand or eye
Dare frame thy fearful symmetry?

– WILLIAM BLAKE (1757-1827)

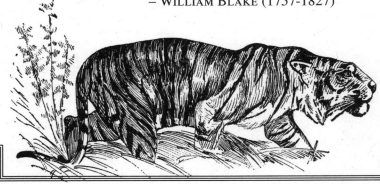

Yesterday, Today and Tomorrow

RUSSIAN PAGANS. Sometimes a cluster of pagans turns up in surprising places. In the Volga region of Mari-El, a republic  under Russian control, locals carry on rituals passed down by distant ancestors. Somehow Christianity never took root deep in the birch-laden forests of these remote villages – little has changed from the dimmest reaches of centuries. Here people still gather in groves to worship in the manner of the ancients, intent on honoring ancestors and nature. Men and women wear the traditional regional costumes, white dresses and tunics embroidered in red. The Maris pay tribute to a pantheon of gods, the most notable the Great White God, the God of Wind and the God of Fire. The sect also worships many half men/half gods, Chumbulat the most venerated, a guardian and warrior believed to dwell on a Mari-El

mountain. Some strong forces, and political powers, nudge the culture – but if push comes to shove, we would bet rubles on the cultural survival of the tenacious Maris.

THE WEIRD SISTERS. Macbeth has never lost its spooky appeal. This year as for every year, productions of the blood-spattered tragedy turn up all over the world. The three witches ever stir the cauldron, continuing their subtly diabolical assault on the man who would be king. They predict Macbeth's rise to the throne that tempts  him toward evil. Shakespeare, a good countryman, was familiar with herbs sometimes used in witchcraft. Banquo mentions an "insane root," a plant causing madness, believed to refer to henbane or hemlock. Shakespeare knew that the play would have enormous appeal to King James, the author of *Daemonology*, enthralled with necromancy. The monarch wrote that witches "can rayse stormes and tempests in the aire." The tragedy is notorious for the number of actors injured in its productions. As a result the "M" word is only spoken on stage;

it is otherwise "the Scottish play." If a cast member gets orally careless in the dressing room, he must reverse the curse – run from the building, turn three times, spit and ask permission to reenter the theater and continue.

MAYAN CHEERS! For years anthropologist Patricia Crown puzzled over unique cylindrical clay jars unearthed in the ruins at Chaco Canyon, New Mexico. The site, built by Pueblo ancestors, is a complex of multistory housing arising from the mesa. The vessels were decorated with hieroglyphics and beautifully depicted Mayan court scenes. Crown knew that beans and corn had spread north of Mexico, and perhaps other trade products. Some scholars believed that the jars were topped with stretched skins and used as drums or made to store sacred objects. On a hunch Crown submitted shards to the Hershey lab and tested for traces of

cacao. As suspected, the jars originally had held liquid chocolate – more than 1,200 miles from the nearest cacao tree. The beans were fermented, roasted, ground, mixed with water and flavorings and whipped into a froth. The drink was obviously a luxury, doubtless used for ceremonial occasions. "It's as if you were having a dinner party and serving really nice Champagne," states a museum curator. "You serve Champagne in really nice glasses."

SHAMAN GRAVE ODDITIES. Israeli archaeologists had never seen such a strangely elaborate burial. In a dig near the Sea of Galilee, they exposed a twelve-thousand-year-old skeleton, her skull resting on a tortoise shell. Within the oval grave were arranged forty-nine other tortoise shells, a leopard pelvis, a cow tail and part of an eagle's wing. The skeleton was the body of a deformed 45-year-old woman from the Natufian tribe, hunter-gatherers scattered at that time from Syria to the Sinai. Archaeologists believe that the bones

are that of a witch doctor or shaman, defined by the artifacts and position of burial. The theory is also advanced by her infirmity, which would have caused a limp. Natufians believed that shamans communicated with animal spirits, especially people with unusual bodies. The skeleton was covered with several rocks, perhaps to keep the spirit entombed. The grave also contained a mortar and pestle, doubtless to grind components for spells.

JELLYFISH GROWING DOWN.

Apparently we all grow older except movie stars from the Botox School of Dramatic Arts and certain jellyfish. *Turritopsis dohrnii*, the size of a human fingernail, has the ability to transform itself from adult to baby when threatened. Even more amazing, in emergencies they can process the same age change again and again. The jellyfish reproduce in the usual way of sperm and eggs. But on the brink of death from starvation or injury, the jellyfish becomes a transparent cyst

which develops into a their first stage of life. In yet another unique transformation, muscle cells may become nerve cells or even sperms and eggs. Marine biologists have recently discovered this genetic key to the growing fleet of a worldwide "invasive jellyfish swarm."

GOOD TO BE THE KING. In 1997 photographer Thomas Harbin founded Wallachia, a fantasy domain north of Prague, not to be confused with an actual area in Romania. Harbin established a king, a famous actor and clown, thereafter known as Bolak I, the Kind-Hearted Forever. The country became an elaborate practical joke cherished by the Czechs. Wallachian locals tended to drink 110-proof plum brandy for breakfast, relished black humor and airy fantasy. Amused visitors flocked to the site as the zany kingdom assumed trappings of statehood, including wheat-backed currency and a Navy of 40

canoes. Tourist euros surged in. King Bolak Polivka took his role seriously, signing passports, selling consulates and demanding one million Czech crowns to remain enthroned. Harbin, serving as foreign minister, took a dim view. He toppled Bolak and declared a construction worker the new king. The coup wound up in court. A real one. The judge ruled that Polivka could not profit from any association with the kingdom. The Kind-Hearted Forever seemed undeterred, according to the *Times*: "There is an air force loyal to me, a royal guard; we even have a tank division," Polivka stated. "We have not only conquered space but planted our sacred blue plum trees on the moon."

IRON AGE LINGO. Language experts rejoiced in an extraordinary find this year, a large, rough, yellowish tablet inscribed in a bygone Iberian language, Southwest Script. The discovery offered eighty-six characters, the longest Iron Age text ever unearthed. About ninety such slate tablets in smaller sizes have been discovered since the eighteenth century, scattered around Portugal and in the Andalusia area of Spain. What drives linguists crazy is the dissimilar appearance of the letters. Some are just squiggles like doodles, some look like crossed sticks, one looks like a bow tie, another looks like a number four. The writing is a joined letter-to-letter script reading from right to left, dating from between 2,500 and 2,800 years ago. Who chiseled these messages into the mysterious stones? What did they say? Theories abound, but no one knows for sure. According to Professor

Pierre Swiggers, University of Leuven, Belgium, "Researchers are handicapped because they are peering into a period of history about which they know little. We hardly know anything about the people's daily habits or religious beliefs." Southwest Script is one of a few other ancient languages retrieved from the earth about which the modern world even now remains clueless.

The Calico Cat

Furry collage of conundrums

CALICO CATS have long enjoyed a connection with the weird and offbeat. The dignified tuxedo cat; the legendary status of luck and magic enjoyed by felines of pure white or black; the playful tiger stripes and Garfield-like confidence of the orange marmalade – all are dear to cat fanciers. However none of these can match the eccentric mix in both temperament and appearance of the calico.

A kitty with a coat of at least three different colors, calicos are almost always female. They can resemble a furry crazy-patch quilt covered with random splotches of orange, black, white and even brown or gray. Sometimes the effect is truly ugly. In other cases a calico will have a unique beauty all its own. Beautiful or grotesque, the calico cat's outer appearance of confusion reflects the inner personality and psyche. Its behavior is crazed to the point that many observers are convinced that the cat is truly insane. Perhaps this gives rise to the ill omens linked to calicos. Some years ago U.S. Attorney General John Ashcroft reportedly became agitated when he spotted a calico cat watching him. The incident occurred outside Ashcroft's hotel in The Netherlands just before an important meeting. He was certain that the cat was a harbinger of impending chaos.

The term calico cat was adopted from the name of a whimsical fabric. In earlier times printed cotton cloth was called calico. Colorful, casual and comfortable, it provided an alternative to the more formal and expensive linens, wools and silks. Perhaps the name provides the clue to understanding and appreciating the unique spirit of the calico. Individual, unpredictable and interesting, the calico cat is in harmony with the human urge to relax and be ourselves, oblivious to the demands and expectations of the rest of the world.

– ESTHER ELAYNE

Pilgrimages

Journeys to the sacred

There is that in man that which is divine, and man will be satisfied with nothing less. The pilgrimage is both necessary and impossible.

— ARISTOTLE,
Nicomachean Ethics

IT IS THE human condition to want more from life. We all have felt the call. Yet our daily routines and responsibilities become so ingrained that we forget they are not essential to our being. When we seem ensnared by daily life, it is time to consider a pilgrimage. Such an endeavor is symbolic of our soul's journey toward death and eternity, the journey more important than the destination. The pilgrim is an essential and universal archetype in human consciousness, and the term means "wanderer, traveler or stranger." It derives from *peregre*, Latin for "abroad" or literally, "beyond the boundaries of the field." Not long ago land was marked by boundary stones and all that ventured beyond them were wanderers and explorers. A pilgrimage is a journey beyond the boundaries of everyday life.

Preparation for it begins with a goal. From that, the route and destination can be determined. Many of us already have a destination in mind. In that case, we ask ourselves what we are seeking to realize by reaching it. Goals may be to honor our ancestors, culture or country; to heal; to experience a miracle; to come closer to a deity or pantheon; to assimilate the qualities of a hero we wish to emulate; to achieve a vision; to understand what we want from life.

Sacred rites, sacred times

The goal defines the pilgrim's route. By appealing to the "spirit of place" one

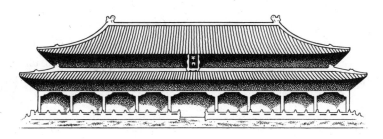

might trigger experiences similar to what has occurred there before. Destinations could include sites of miraculous events, evil events and suffering that changed the world, places of worship, tracing an extraordinary person's life to the tomb, natural locales with special qualities, manmade wonders to behold, a pantheon's mythical dwelling place.

The world doesn't lack sacred places. The desire to reanimate our spirit by communing at a sacred place in a sacred time makes the pilgrim a participant in living mythology. Visiting sacred sites during sacred times hearkens back to an age when humankind venerated nature and believed in the universe's soul. Gods, demigods and spirits were known to inhabit these sacred places, each equipped with specific powers that might occur at specific times of the year – and some could strip away evil deeds and cleanse polluted souls. Being open to the experience is the only essential. One must allow a metamorphosis to occur. Pilgrimage is about moving toward deity.

Three stages
Some religions expect worshipers to make a pilgrimage at least once in their lives. Required or not, the pilgrimage is surely a rite of passage. Anthropologist Arnold Van Gennep interprets the event in three stages: separating from social conditions; separating from normal life to a nominal existence; rejoining life (under its former or new conditions).

After determining one's goal and destination, preparations for separation need to be made. The Japanese poet Basho made ready by selling his worldly goods. He was advanced in age and didn't intend to return. The ritual pilgrimage can be long (although not nearly so long as the ritual of life). Rituals yield their best results undertaken mindfully. The pilgrimage begins by an announcement of intent, especially important for a journey of short duration.

In setting comfort and security aside, pilgrims declare themselves as such, in that way opening themselves to the transcendent and unexpected. Hindus have traditionally made offerings to Ganesh, the god of beginning and overcoming difficulties at this time. Others on the road sing daily hymns to Pu-san to preside over their journey. Each

13

pilgrim marks the beginning with a meaningful offering, such as a poem, prayer, song or flower. Then the journey commences as the pilgrim crosses the threshold into the world beyond.

Outward bound

It is time to venture outside everyday boundaries and become acquainted with the world and one's place in it. As past assumptions drop, the unknown opens to those that are alert and aware. It is

time to hear the world's tales and seek the spirits of a well, a grove, a cave or a mountaintop. At times one may lose confidence and feel alienated or painfully aware of the human condition. One's initial objective may be buried in doubt. This is when the pilgrim needs Basho's words from *The Narrow Road to the Deep North*, "No matter what we may be doing at a given moment, we must not forget that it has a bearing upon our everlasting self which is poetry."

Sometimes a pilgrim must simply take the next step. In the moment, one step added to the others may be all that is manageable. Still, it is that necessary step that leads to the completion of the pilgrimage. Again Basho says it best, "Go outward to find what's inside."

Perhaps one will experience mythologist Patricia Monaghan's discovery circling Ireland: "Going left or right depended on which foot you were on when you came to the crossroads….It is my poet's circuit, circling the island with my left shoulder to the sea, repeating the stories I learned in my travels…. All are relative to the speaker, for the center is 'here' – wherever we stand, orienting ourselves to the world, centers of a compass whose center is everywhere. But the center being everywhere is not the same as the center being nowhere – far from it. The center is not outside us."

Let us begin by remembering the Oracle of Delphi's advice to those who asked, "What is best for man?" or "How can I live most happily?"

"Know thyself."

– NIALLA NI MACHA

CROSSROADS

Thresholds for the strange, alluring, dangerous

LEGENDARY BLUESMAN Robert Johnson is rumored to have sold his soul to the devil. On a crossroads outside Robinsonville, Mississippi, Johnson supposedly met a large black man who took Johnson's guitar, tuned it and handed it back in exchange for his soul. With such recordings as "Cross Roads Blues," "Hellhound on My Tail" and "Me and the Devil Blues," Johnson perpetuated this tale without confirming it. We do know that Johnson left Robinsonville in 1931 as a fair guitarist. But between 1936 and 1938, he recorded twenty-nine songs from which Eric Clapton dubbed him "the most important blues musician that ever lived."

Harry Middleton Hyatt, an Anglican minister and folklorist, believes the Dark Man that Johnson met was not the Judeo-Christian "Satan," but a clearly recognizable vodoun deity known as "Legba." One aspect of Legba is "Kalfu" or "Carrefour" – literally "crossroads."

Trading one's soul is not typical of vodoun rites, nor do they conclude with hell-fire punishments. The crossroad spirit commonly teaches the sought-after skill for payment of a silver coin or simply reappearing for a set number of nights.

The god of one religion often becomes the devil of the next, so it's not surprising that Legba is commonly confused with the Judeo-Christian devil. As a mediator between humankind and the inhabitants of the upper and lower worlds, Legba is the first and last power invoked in a rite. He protects travelers, teaches skills, grants fortune and misfortune. "Papa Legba," it is said, speaks all languages and can help the lost find their way.

Crossroads are characteristically a place for liminal contacts, the term indicating unusual thresholds. Threshold experiences can be psychological or physical, dissolving or relaxing an identity so transition can be made to a newfound understanding, behavior or perspective. One way to banish evil is to sweep an intersection at midnight on a full moon.

Gallows, ghosts, witchcraft and vampires are liminal contacts also associated with crossroads. Until relatively recently, British crossroads were burial places for felons and suicides that witches could reanimate after dark.

As recently as 1823, a body deemed likely to walk after death was impaled with a stake through the heart or navel. Curiously "dod" or "ded" in Anglo Saxon means both "boundary" and "dead." Similarly "witch" translates to "hedge rider" – where boundaries between farms are commonly marked with hedges.

The god forms met at crossroads are typically tricksters and psychopomps, conductors of dead souls. In this light it is foreseeable that Persephone's guides to and from Elysium are Hermes, the herald, and Hecate, the torchbearer. Hermes and Hecate received a majority of the appeals in Greek magical papyri and curse tablets, found at ancient crossroads. Hermes was honored with "herms," likeness in stone, for his mediations between gods and man. Hecate as Goddess of Witches, Queen of Ghosts and Keeper of the Keys was honored with masks mounted on poles to gaze down each path where three roads meet.

The crossroads is more than a meeting point on the horizontal plane. It's a sacred center linking the heavens and underworld. An equal armed cross symbolizes this intersection where the elements of life distill into a single point.

Italian cities were once built with *templums* marking a city's center under which a cave or *mundus* was dug to receive each year's first fruits. This gateway to the underworld was unsealed ritualistically three times a year to give underworld spirits access to the world of man.

In Royston a standing stone and *mundus* in the ancient British town still mark a crossroads oriented to the four cardinal directions. This "Roy" stone may have been the "King" stone from which an ancient king ruled. In the cave beneath it, Saint Catherine is depicted as a Christianized Queen of the Underworld. Similarly Legba is sometimes identified with Saint Anthony, patron of travelers.

Being at the "center of the world" can empower one to choose from the infinite potential awaiting us. Robert Johnson's tale illustrates just how these crossroads continue to carry a reputation for the strange, alluring and dangerous. Their power is seductive, alluring and dangerous – and can be the sacred key to unlock the threshold between worlds.

– LILLIAN GENTRY

The Glass Harmonica

Weird instrument, weird sound

RENAISSANCE Faires, which provide a wonderful foray into the magical universe, are one of the venues where the haunting sound of a little-known musical instrument can be enjoyed. More and more frequently the glass harmonica sings in the background, delighting those who would follow the Old Ways. The player uses a series of glass bowls or goblets, usually combined with water, to produce sounds by way of friction.

Try your own basic version. Partly fill a wineglass with water. Wet your finger and rub it along the rim. Now you are playing a one-note glass harmonica. The sound it emits can seem ethereal, even disorienting. That's because the predominant sound range produced is delicate. To some listeners the tones created by the water rubbing glass sound angelic; the instrument has even been called the "voice of angels." To others it sounds like a cacophony of hellish noise. The glass harmonica has also been nicknamed a "ghost fiddle," and thought to have the ability to awaken the dead if played at midnight. At one time when an important event occurred it was said that the glass harmonica played. People believed that the instrument opened the gates of heaven as well as hell with sounds either too close to the voices of angels to please God or too demonic to be heard outside the fiery pit of doomsday.

In favor, out of favor

The glass harmonica was also called the "armonica," a word derived from the root word for "harmony," documented during the Renaissance. The instrument has also been called the "bowl organ" and "hydro-crystalophone." Galileo considered the potential of sound created by water in his book, *Two New Sciences*. Richard Puckeridge, an eighteenth-century Irish musician, was a well-known early player. He was the first to perform in London with an instrument composed of glass vessels filled with variable amounts of water. Puckeridge and his unusual program created a sensation.

The instrument fell out of favor late in the nineteenth century. Claims were made that the glass harmonica's

melodious yet strange tone would cause both musicians and the audience to go mad. Noted musicologists in Germany even stated that the instrument caused death through excessively stimulating on the nerves and generating melancholy and self-doubt. The manager of armonica player Marianne Kirchgessner, in her 1809 obituary, even blamed the glass music for her untimely demise at the age of thirty-nine. Other claims were made that touching the glass with wet fingers would cause death and insanity due to poisoning from the lead in the glass. No scientific basis has been found to support this theory.

Franklin invents his own

Benjamin Franklin was one devoted glass harmonica player who lived to a ripe old age and certainly was not driven mad by the music. The ever-inventive Franklin created an ingenious treadle-operated version of the instrument. He used over thirty glass bowls mounted on a spindle turned by a foot pedal as water was stroked by hand onto the glass. Different colors of paint on the rims showed which specific notes would play; A's were dark blue, B's purple, C's red, D's orange, E's yellow, F's green, G's light blue. Flats and sharps were white. Students of yoga and tarot will notice the color and musical correlations with both the chakras and Major Arcana. Psychologist Franz Mesmer recognized the value of the glass harmonica to induce a deep state of trance, a tool he used in his studies of mesmerism.

Renowned composers, including Mozart, Beethoven, Saint-Saëns and Strauss wrote music especially for the glass harmonica. Tchaikovsky's first draft of "Dance of the Sugar Plum Fairy" from the Nutcracker ballet called for a glass harmonica, although the composer later dropped the instrument from the score. European monarchs played it, most notably Marie Antoinette.

Revival

Tainted by superstition and overwhelmed by competition from more modern instruments, the glass harmonica suddenly fell from favor and nearly vanished by the late nineteenth century. A few original armonicas survived into the twentieth, when revival began slowly. In the 1930's Bruno Hoffman, a German virtuoso, presented a repertoire of stunning performances using his "glass harp," an instrument fashioned from of a series of wine-glasses in a box. In 1952 two French artists, Bernard and François Baschet, invented what they called a "crystal organ," made of glass rods.

In 1975 the Bakken Museum in Minneapolis purchased one of Franklin's remaining armonicas from an instrument dealer in France.

The display sparked more interest in vintage instruments. In 1984 a master glass blower and musician from Massachusetts, Gerhard B. Finkbeiner, began to produce glass armonicas again commercially. An impressive word, hydrodaktulopsycicarmonica, has been coined recently, referring to the instruments with approximate Greek roots for water, fingers and psyche/soul.

Although Finkbeiner passed away in 1999 at the age of sixty-nine, his work lives on. A small but devoted and growing group of contemporary musicians play otherworldly tunes on various prototypes of the glass harmonica. The husband-and-wife team of Glass Music, Eric Paul and Susan Scites, are notable adherents. Using water in glasses placed on a table, they have produced several wonderful CD's of glass harmonica music. The Scites frequently perform at Renaissance Faires and can be reached at www.fairewynds.com.

– ESTHER ELAYNE

Armonica

Adagio & Rondo

W. A. Mozart
K. 617, completed Vienna, May 23, 1791

Hachiko

Icon of unswerving faith

IN 1994 the Culture Network Station in Japan was able to lift a recording of a dog barking from an old record broken into several pieces. The achievement received fanfare in the media, and on Saturday, May 28, the station broadcast the sound. Millions of Japanese tuned in to hear Hachiko bark, the dog still in their hearts fifty-nine years after his death. Then as now Hachiko is famous for his remarkable fidelity, a revered quality the Japanese identify with family spirit.

Born in Akita province in 1923, at the age of one year the dog joined his master, Eisaburo Ueno. The pair enjoyed each other enormously right from the start. Ueno lived in the Shibuya area of Tokyo and was a professor at the Imperial University. Every morning Hachiko accompanied his master to the busy train station, set amid flashing neon signs, clustered shops and scurrying commuters. Every afternoon at three o'clock the dog would wait patiently amid the bedlam, tail wagging furiously at the first sign of his master's return. But the happy routine came to an abrupt end a year later. The professor had suffered a stroke and died while in a classroom at the university.

The long vigil

Although Hachiko was less than two years old, the affinity between dog and owner was so powerful it remained lifelong for the single abiding partner. Each day the dog, now known as Chu-ken Hachiko (the faithful dog Hachiko), kept his vigil at the Shibuya Station. He waited, he watched. Sometimes he stayed for days at a time, not returning home. "Faithful dog Hachiko" kept to the same agenda for ten years. Commuters left him food and water. Countless media stories acquainted all of Japan with Hachiko. He died on March 7, 1935, at the very spot where he had always hoped for a reunion with his beloved master. A day of national mourning marked the death of Chu-ken Hachiko, canine symbol of loyalty.

Hachiko remembered

A year before his passing, people who saw Hachiko every day were so touched that they banded together and raised money for a statue at the station. Andu Tero, a famous Japanese sculptor, created a fine bronze, and the aging Hachiko was on hand for the unveiling.

The statue was melted down for recycling during World War II; after the war people still missed the statue. But the original artist had died, and in 1948 his son was commissioned to make a second bronze. The statue has become a landmark rendezvous spot, meeting place for friends and pilgrimage for tourists. People pet Hachiko's head out of affection or for luck. Travelers can buy souvenirs of their favorite canine at the Hachiko Memorial Store and a large mosaic of Akitas at play adorns a wall of the station.

In 1987 a Japanese film-maker produced the lovely *Hachiko Monogatari*, the dog's story from birth to death, including a ghostly reunion with his master. Lasse Hallstrom (*Chocolat, The Ciderhouse Rules*) created a semi-fictional American remake with Richard Gere as the Japanese professor. Hachiko also turns up as the subject of a 2004 children's book, *The True Story of a Loyal Dog*, by Pamela S. Turner, beautifully illustrated by Yan Nascimbene. *Hachiko Waits*, a short novel "for all ages" came out the same year, by Leslea Newman, illustrated by Machiyo Kodaira. The dog also turns up in a Nintendo game and in a Pokemon episode.

For the Japanese people, the iconic canine lives on in form and fur. Mounted by a taxidermist, the dog's remains are on view at the National Science Museum in Tokyo. Hachiko still seems to be waiting on the alert, forever hopeful, forever the symbol of fidelity revered by the Japanese.

Bronze Hachiko still waits at the station

Mayan Calendar Prophecy

December 21, 2012

A new Golden Age?

EXTREME weather, political upheaval, incredible economic concerns and other changes in the familiar world all unfold before our eyes daily. Nothing seems the same any more. Comfort can be found in remembering that these times have been predicted for hundreds of years. A deeper meaning prevails behind the current events that appear so challenging. The wise, those who follow the Old Ways of the witch, must focus on creating the magic to assure a positive outcome for all. Within the pages of *The Witches' Almanac* guidance can be found. Seek in order to discover that the path to well being and a bright future begins right here.

The Mayan Calendar, along with the parallel prophecies of Nostradamus, Edgar Cayce, the Egyptian pyramid calendar, Mother Shipton, the Book of Revelations and the Hopi Elders, suggests that life on Earth will go through a complete catharsis during the early twenty-first century. The date of December 21, 2012, coinciding with the winter solstice, is clearly shown in the records left by the Maya as an important time for humanity.

The ancient Maya were an indigenous Native American people who lived in Central America between the Tropic of Cancer and the Equator. Today the Yucatan peninsula and other parts of Mexico, Belize, Honduras, El Salvador and Guatemala bear traces of the impressive Maya culture. When London was merely a tiny, miserable outpost of the Roman Empire, over fifty thousand people flourished in ancient Tikal. They were housed in palaces with hundreds of rooms or in comfortable homes built around plazas. The Maya created a sophisticated civilization that seems to have predated the Egyptian culture and Stonehenge before inexplicably disappearing between 1500 and 900 B.C.E. – an era that predated the arrival of the Spanish conquistadors. The Maya left behind silent tributes with encoded messages in the form of numerous massive stone structures that remain rising above the mists of dense jungle foliage.

The encoded messages are of great importance to those who seek to understand what is really happening right now. The interpretation of celestial patterns of time, astrology, is part of this. Through using a counting technique and establishing miraculous accuracy in mathematics and astronomy, combined with deep trance states or meditation, the Maya were able to accurately predict times for planting crops, confronting enemies and making personal decisions. They had readers among them, much as people today seek information from astrologers and psychics.

Celestial information was inscribed on buildings, including pyramids. The pyramids were also used for energy transmission and rituals.

About twenty different calendars (think of them as almanacs) were developed. The Moon's 28-day cycle, the orbit of Venus which correlates with the 260-day human gestation cycle, a solar year of 365 days and other almanacs were established. They all were a part of a greater cycle, which was composed of five ages of humanity. Today's astrologers call this the Great Year. The Great Year is the time our Sun takes to orbit the Galactic Center of the Milky Way. It is the series of world ages as marked by the precession of the equinoxes. It is our Sun encircling a greater more distant sun. This takes about twenty-six thousand years. It is completed when the winter solstice sunrise aligns with the Galactic Center. Both a finale and a new beginning are marked. December 21, 2012 is Earth's due date with next alignment with the Galactic Center, most scholars concur.

At key times marked within the Great Year the dinosaurs vanished. The Ice Age began. The Neanderthal or Stone Age people disappeared and Cro Magnon, a modern humanoid, appeared. Indicators suggest a link to the destruction of Atlantis. Refugees from an ancient golden culture escaped to Egypt, Europe and the Yucatan to gradually begin civilization all over again. Details and timing are hazy, the accuracy and clarity of specifics are shrouded by time, but something major definitely happened. Scientists agree that the timing of prehistoric events on Earth isn't as definite as formerly thought.

Is this all a myth or is it today's reality show? Only time will tell. A positive outlook, faith in the greater universal good and flexibility are the tools needed. Think of it as a special challenge and a privilege to be a part of the elite generation of people who will usher out an old and familiar era to welcome a new Great Age.

– DIKKI-JO MULLEN

MOON GARDENING

BY PHASE

Sow, transplant, bud and graft | *Plow, cultivate, weed and reap*

NEW	First Quarter	FULL	Last Quarter	NEW
Plant above-ground crops with outside seeds, flowering annuals.	Plant above-ground crops with inside seeds.	Plant root crops, bulbs, biennials, perennials.		Do not plant.

BY PLACE IN THE ZODIAC

Fruitful Signs

Cancer—Most favorable planting time for all leafy crops bearing fruit above ground. Prune to encourage growth in Cancer.

Scorpio—Second only to Cancer, a Scorpion Moon promises good germination and swift growth. In Scorpio, prune for bud development.

Pisces—Planting in the last of the Watery Triad is especially effective for root growth.

Taurus—The best time to plant root crops is when the Moon is in the sign of the Bull.

Capricorn—The Earthy Goat Moon promotes the growth of rhizomes, bulbs, roots, tubers and stalks. Prune now to strengthen branches.

Libra—Airy Libra may be the least beneficial of the Fruitful Signs, but is excellent for planting flowers and vines.

Barren Signs

Leo—Foremost of the Barren Signs, the Lion Moon is the best time to effectively destroy weeds and pests. Cultivate and till the soil.

Gemini—Harvest in the Airy Twins; gather herbs and roots. Reap when the Moon is in a sign of Air or Fire to assure best storage.

Virgo—Plow, cultivate, and control weeds and pests when the moon is in Virgo.

Sagittarius—Plow and cultivate the soil or harvest under the Archer Moon. Prune now to discourage growth.

Aquarius—This dry sign of Air is perfect for ground cultivation, reaping crops, gathering roots and herbs. It is a good time to destroy weeds and pests.

Aries—Cultivate, weed, and prune to lessen growth. Gather herbs and roots for storage.

Consult our Moon Calendar pages for phase and place in the zodiac circle. The Moon remains in a sign for about two-and-a-half days. Match your gardening activity to the day that follows the Moon's entry into that zodiac sign.

The MOON Calendar

is divided into zodiac signs rather than the more familiar Gregorian calendar.

2010

2011

Bear in mind that new projects should be initiated when the Moon is waxing (from dark to full); when the Moon is on the wane (from full to dark), it is a time for storing energy and the wise person waits.

Please note that Moons are listed by day of entry into each sign. Quarters are marked, but as rising and setting times vary from one region to another, it is advisable to check your local newspaper, library or planetarium.

The Moon's Place is computed for Eastern Standard Time.

⇥ Looking Back ⇤

Collectors always discover the pleasure of browsing their back issues of The Witches' Almanac, *replete with fascinating features. Our new annual offering looks back at our own favorites from years past. The beautiful commentary below is by an eleventh-century Iranian teacher, philosopher and wandering ascetic, originally published in the 1975/1976 Almanac.*

Sufi Dance

A PURELY RELIGIOUS use of music and dancing is that of the Sufis, who by this means stir up in themselves greater love towards the deity, and often obtain spiritual visions and ecstasies, their hearts becoming in this condition as clean as silver in the flame of a furnace, and attaining a degree of purity which could never be attained by any amount of mere outward austerities. The Sufi then becomes so keenly aware of his relationship to the spiritual world that he loses all consciousness of this world, and often falls down senseless.

Music and dancing fan into a flame whatever love is dormant in the heart, whether it be earthly or sensual, or divine and spiritual. Therefore if a man has in his heart that inner love which the law enjoins it is perfectly lawful for him to take part in the exercises which promote it. On the other hand, if his heart is full of sensual desires, music and dancing will only increase them, and are therefore unlawful for him.

It is not, however, lawful for the aspirant to Sufism to take part in this mystical dancing without the permission of his "Pir," or spiritual director. It is related of the Sheikh Abu'l Qasim Girgani that, when one of his disciples requested leave to take part in such a dance, he said, "Keep a strict fast for three days; then let them cook for you tempting dishes; if, then, you still prefer the dance, you may take part in it." The disciple, however, whose heart is not thoroughly purged from earthly desires, though he may have obtained some glimpse of the mystic's path, should be forbidden by his director to take part in such dances, as they will do him more harm than good.

– *The Alchemy of Happiness*,
Muhammad ibn Muhammad Abu Hamid Al-Ghazali (1058-1111 C.E.)

capricorn

December 21 – January 19

Cardinal Sign of Earth ♍ Ruled by Saturn ♄

S	M	T	W	T	F	S
	Dec. 21 Winter Solstice ⊙	22 *Watch the sunrise* Pisces	23	24 Aries	25 *Rod Serling born, 1924*	26 *Enjoy the scent of pine*
27 Taurus	28	29 *Stay warm* Gemini	30 *Partial ⇨ lunar eclipse*	31 Wolf Moon Cancer	Jan. 1 2010 WANING	2 *Smile often* Leo
3	4 *Blessings from old to new* Virgo	5	6 Libra	7	8 *Drink hot chocolate* Scorpio	9 Feast of Janus
10 *Tell a story*	11 Sagittarius	12	13 *Dispel a nightmare* Capricorn	14 *Partial ⇨ solar eclipse*	15	16 WAXING Aquarius
17	18 *A.A. Milne born, 1882* Pisces	19 *Watch and wait*				

thyme

Place thyme in your pillowcase to bring dreams of the future and repel nightmares. Burn it to purge a room of evil influences.

– Magic Charms from A to Z

The Frog That Wouldn't Laugh

FROGS OFTEN connect to the deluge myths found everywhere. In Australia the aborigines say that a vast frog once drank all the water in the world and caused great drought and misery. If they could only make the frog laugh, they reasoned, he would expel the water. Several of the animals cavorted about acting silly, but the unamused frog kept his huge mouth clamped. Then an eel wriggled in a giddy dance. The frog roared with laughter, and the water poured forth again to refresh the earth and restore life.

— BARBARA STACY, *Magical Creatures*

aquarius

January 20 – February 18

Fixed Sign of Air △ Ruled by Uranus ♅

S	M	T	W	T	F	S
Fennel is believed to have brought victory to the Greek warriors. — Magic Charms from A to Z			Jan. 20	21 Aries	22 Rupert Gleadow born, 1909	23 ◐ Taurus
24	25 Start the day with laughter Gemini	26 Hans Holzer born, 1920	27 Cancer	28	29 Express love Leo	30 Storm Moon
31 WANING Gone but not forgotten Virgo	Feb. 1 Oimelc Eve	2 Candlemas Libra	3 Write a poem	4 Scorpio	5 Turn a coin	6 ◑
7 Sagittarius	8 Carry adventure	9 Forgive a hurt Capricorn	10	11	12 Practice invisibility Aquarius	13 Year of the Tiger
14 WAXING Pisces	15 Love deeply Lupercalia	16 Embrace wisdom	17	18 The answer will surface Aries	FENNEL	

The pouder of the seed of Fennell drunke for certaine daies together fasting preserveth the eye-sight.

— Gerard's Herbal (1597)

The Ant and the Dove

AN ANT went to a river to quench its thirst, and being carried away by the rush of the stream was on the point of drowning. A Dove sitting on a tree overhanging the water plucked a leaf and let it fall into the water close to her. The Ant climbed onto it and floated in safety to the bank. Shortly afterwards a bird-catcher came and stood under the tree, and laid his lime-twigs for the Dove, which sat in its branches. The Ant, perceiving his design, stung him in the foot. In pain the birdcatcher threw down the twigs, and the noise made the Dove take wing.

Moral: One good turn deserves another.

pisces

February 19 – March 20

Mutable Sign of Water ▽ Ruled by Neptune ♆

S	M	T	W	T	F	S
The decoction of Turneps is good against the cough and hoarsenesse of the voice, being drunke in the evening with a little sugar, or a quantitie of clarified hony. — Gerard's Herbal (1597)					FEB. **19** Copernicus born, 1473	**20** Taurus
21 Gemini	**22**	**23** Gossip abounds	**24** Wilhelm Grimm born, 1786 Cancer	**25**	**26** Favor a cat Leo	**27**
28 Chaste Moon Virgo	MARCH **1** WANING Matronalia	**2** Libra	**3** Sing to the goddesses	**4** Scorpio	**5**	**6** Sagittarius
7	**8** Dream of the sea	**9** Capricorn	**10**	**11** Wear something blue Aquarius	**12**	**13**
14 Daylight Savings Time begins @ 2am Pisces	**15**	**16** WAXING Aries	**17** Wash thresholds	**18** Buy seeds Taurus	**19** Minerva's Day	**20**

TURNIP

The Turnep it selfe being stamped, is with good successe applied upon mouldy or kibed heeles, and that also oile of Roses boiled in a hollow turnep under the hot embers doth cure the same.
— Gerard's Herbal (1597)

Duende

The dark side of inspiration

A DUENDE, from the Spanish "dueño" or "owner," is a character from mythology, similar to what we term a goblin, elf or fairy. The duendes are dark spirits with a reputation for mischief, capable of possessing the unsuspecting. Duendes have been known to hide important objects, cause young women to become lost in the woods, and even steal the toes of sleeping children. Such spirits live in forests or inside the walls of rural homes, where they wait for their chance to cause trouble.

Beyond the mythological creatures, the term "duende" has crucial meaning, especially to artists in southern Spain and especially to performing artists. Duende is an elusive quality that implies dark inspiration. Possessed by duende, the artist is capable of creating work that evokes immediate powerful reactions in spectators. Performers who have technical command of their craft, yet without passion or emotion, are said to "lack duende" – the maniacal, almost diabolical energy that blazes from truly moving art. While the muse drives artists through a recognition of the vibrant living world, duende drives the artist through a confrontation with death. Duende reminds the artist of her temporal nature and imminent passing, urging her onward because there is not much time left. Suppressing and dismissing the rational faculties, duende seizes both the artist and the audience on a visceral plane, demanding that they surrender to the intensity of such music, dance or spoken poetry.

While harnessing the duende can contribute raw power to a work of art, artists who seek the duende should be forewarned – duendes possess only those who already have a measure of darkness deep within their souls.

– SHANNON MARKS

Aubrey Beardsley, 1893

aries

March 20 – April 19
Cardinal Sign of Fire △ Ruled by Mars ♂

S	M	T	W	T	F	S
RAM *On a steep cliff hill in Algeria where the Sahara Desert meets the Atlas Mountains is a remarkable engraving made over 7,000 years ago. An enormous ram towers over a man whose arms are rased as if in awe.* – Magical Creatures						Mar. **20** 2010 Vernal Equinox Taurus
21 Gemini	**22** *William Shatner born, 1931*	**23** Cancer	**24**	**25** Be a leader Leo	**26** Have a party	**27** Order your life Virgo
28 Plant seeds indoors	**29** Seed Moon Libra	**30** WANING	**31**	April **1** All Fools' Day Scorpio	**2** Tell a joke	**3** Sagittarius
4	**5** Capricorn	**6**	**7** Change a pattern Aquarius	**8**	**9** Lady luck visits	**10** Joan Quigley born, 1927 Pisces
11	**12** Think peaceful thoughts	**13** Aries	**14**	**15** WAXING Taurus	**16** Toss a pebble into water	**17** Gemini
18	**19** Cancer	*The great god Amon, whose worship combined with power of the Sun god, Ra, claimed the Ram as his symbolic creature.* – Magical Creatures 				

Summer
The Season of Harvest

from Le Rouge's *Grant Kalendrier*, Troyes, 1496

Summer's lease hath all too short a date.
— *William Shakespeare*

taurus

April 20 – May 19

Fixed Sign of Earth ♉ Ruled by Venus ♀

S	M	T	W	T	F	S
CATTLE	April 20	21	22 Leo	23 Hold onto love	24 Carry three pebbles Virgo	
25 Al Pacino born, 1940	26 Carry a flower Libra	27	28 Hare Moon Scorpio	29 WANING	30 Walpurgis Night Sagittarius	May 1 Beltane
2	3 Capricorn	4	5 Write a poem Aquarius	6	7 Start the day with a song	8 White Lotus Day Pisces
9 Use your creativity	10 Aries	11 Discard fears	12 Taurus	13	14 Wear white	15 WAXING Gemini
16 Watch and see	17 Dennis Hopper born, 1936 Cancer	18	19 Pick yellow flowers Leo			

Celtic tribes in Ireland chose their king in an elaborate ceremony called the tarbfeis. A bull was slain, roasted and its meat and broth consumed as musicians played and priests chanted incantations. In the sleep following the feast, a dream would reveal the name of the future king to the presiding druid.

– Magical Creatures

Magpies

Good birds, bad birds

MAGPIES often receive a bad press, perhaps because of an ancient belief that seemed to spring out of nowhere. Some people were convinced that magpies, of all God's creatures, were the only ones to forego the comfort of the interior Ark. They opted for perching by themselves atop the vessel, chattering maliciously at the animals huddled within. Add to this a legend that magpies were the only *Corvidae* refusing to don full mourning dress on the day of Christ's crucifixion. Their kin, ravens and crows, attended in sober black; magpies as usual were pied with white.

From such folklore we can see why these birds are met with some ambivalence. It is considered unlucky to kill magpies, and in certain areas of Europe the birds are honored for the chattering that warns of approaching wolves. In Scotland, however, they are regarded as the Devil's own bird, believed to have an unholy drop of his blood under their tongues. In Scotland and England it is unlucky to see one flying away from the sun. Whoever does so should grab the first object that come to hand, throw it after the bird and say, "Bad luck to the bird that flies widdershins."

Old ways exist believed to avert a malevolent magpie sighting: Raise your hat in salutation. Form a cross with your foot on the ground (or as many crosses as magpies). Wet your forefinger with spittle and make the sign of the cross on your shoe. Spit on the ground three times and say, "Devil, Devil, I defy thee! Magpie, Magpie, I go by thee!"

A single magpie is especially associated with bad luck. Only one bird croaking persistently around a house, for instance, sounds the death knell of an occupant. Two magpies foretell good luck, although it is still necessary to salute the duo by bowing or spitting to ensure that the auspicious omen will be fulfilled.

A childhood rhyme indicates the ambivalent and magical nature of the magpie sightings: One for sorrow/ Two for joy/ Three for a girl/ Four for a boy/ Five for silver/ Six for gold/ Seven for a secret/ Never to be told.

– SARAH SIMPSON ENOCK

gemini

May 20 – June 20

Mutable Sign of Air △ Ruled by Mercury ☿

S	M	T	W	T	F	S
The Greek word "psyche" means both "soul" and "butterfly," and since ancient times the elegant airborne creature has symbolized rebirth. – Magical Creatures				MAY **20** Virgo?	**21** Virgo	**22**
23 Libra	**24** Consult a witch	**25** Scorpio	**26** Vesak Day ⇨	**27** Dyad Moon Sagittarius	**28** WANING	**29** Oak Apple Day
30 Capricorn	**31** Walk in the rain	JUNE **1** Aquarius	**2** Look for a rainbow	**3**	**4** Pisces	**5** Night of the Watchers
6 Aries	**7**	**8** Grant Lewi born, 1902	**9** Taurus	**10** Toss three pennies	**11** Wish on a cloud Gemini	**12**
13 WAXING Cancer	**14** Ask the cards	**15** Leo	**16** Write a friend	**17** Virgo	**18** Read palms	**19**
20 Pick St. Johnswort Libra	**BUTTERFLY** Butterflies also flutter their way into some creation myths. A Sumatran tribe claims descent from three brothers hatched from butterfly eggs. – Magical Creatures					

TAROT'S MOON

THE MOON.

Rider-Waite-Smith deck

The eighteenth card of the Major Arcana, the Moon, shines down on a scene of disquiet below. The face on the right – the side of mercy – reveals displeasure as it contemplates the howling beasts below, a dog and a wolf. The waxing Moon emits 32 rays, 16 major and 15 minor, and casts off 15 drops of lunar moisture, a number associated with birth and thought. In the background loom two towers or tombs. In the foreground, a pond with a crawfish struggling to reach land. Will it fall back and emerge in an eternal struggle? A mysterious path from the water wanders and disappears into the distance.

The card reflects illusion, phobias and fears that thrive in moonlight or reflected light. The dog and wolf, our animal natures, and the creature trying to crawl from the abyss may be eased by the radiance from above. It is the light of knowledge, the lunar "dew of thought," the tears of Isis. The Moon is striving to calm the turbulent forces visible and emerging from the deeps of our own psyches.

cancer
June 21 – July 21
Cardinal Sign of Water ▽ Ruled by Moon ☽

S	M	T	W	T	F	S
CRAB	June **21** Summer Solstice ☼	**22** Scorpio	**23** *Talk to the fairies*	**24** Midsummer Sagittarius	**25** Partial lunar eclipse ⇨	**26** Mead Moon Capricorn
27 WANING	**28** Aquarius	**29** *Antoine de St. Exupéry born, 1900*	**30**	July **1** *Visit the sea* Pisces	**2**	**3** *Pick berries*
4 Aries	**5**	**6** *Make peace* Taurus	**7**	**8** Gemini	**9** *Write a friend*	**10**
11 Cancer	**12** Total solar ⇦ eclipse WAXING	**13** *Express gratitude* Leo	**14**	**15** Virgo	**16** *Befriend a tree*	**17** Libra
18	**19** *Enjoy solitude* Scorpio	**20** *Theda Bara born, 1890*	**21** Sagittarius			

When Hercules was engaged in his horrendous battle with the nine-headed Hydra, Hera sent a sea crab to bite Hercules on the heel. For such obedience, Hera rewarded the crab by placing it in the heavens as a constellation.

– Witches All

金虎

YEAR OF THE METAL TIGER
February 14, 2010 to February 2, 2011

In the Far East, Tiger is a colorful character with a dramatic approach to life. Power, passion, courage and a certain ferociousness make this wildcat a figure of awe and respect combined with a hint of dread. The Tiger's year is a time of boldness and extremes. Expect a few disagreements. Be patient with those who are less than diplomatic. There is rashness afoot in the jungle. Cope by keeping a sense of humor and thinking things through. Those who gamble and take drastic risks can meet with regrets. Succeed instead by stalking Tiger using subtle strategy.

The new, bold and controversial will be introduced by the less than timid Metal Tiger. A fiery heat warms everyone and everything with new vitality. Massive changes are on the horizon. Hope comes to lost causes or previously failed ventures. Relationships are fragile.

The oriental astrology cycle follows a pattern of twelve years. Five elements, fire, water, wood, metal and earth are incorporated in a sixty-year pattern. Then the element-animal pairs repeat. Chinese New Year begins in late January to mid February, at the time of the second New Moon following the winter solstice. This is the New Moon in Aquarius in the familiar western zodiac.

Those born during a Tiger year are vivacious and impulsive. The exciting, vigorous and assertive Tiger is respected for its great energy and originality.

If you were born during one of the Years of the Tiger as listed below, you can anticipate a new cycle of growth and opportunity this year.

1914   1926   1938   1950   1962   1974   1986   1998   2010

Illustration by Ogmios MacMerlin

40

leo

July 22 – August 22
Fixed Sign of Fire △ Ruled by Sun ☉

S	M	T	W	T	F	S
LION *Its mane like tongues of fire, the golden lion is traditionally a beast of the sun.* – Witches All				JULY **22**	**23** Ancient Egyptian New Year Capricorn	**24**
25 Wort Moon Aquarius	**26** WANING	**27** *Look back at accomplishments*	**28** Pisces	**29** Stanton Friedman born, 1934	**30**	**31** Lughnassad Eve Aries
AUGUST **1** Lammas	**2** *Do not hesitate* Taurus	**3**	**4** *Release fears*	**5** Gemini	**6**	**7** Alan Leo born, 1860 Cancer
8 *Turn a card for luck*	**9** Leo	**10** WAXING	**11** *Greet the bees* Virgo	**12**	**13** Diana's Day Libra	**14**
15 Scorpio	**16**	**17** Sagittarius	**18** *Move like the wind*	**19**	**20** Capricorn	**21** *Show sympathy*
22 Aquarius	*Sole occupant of the House of the Sun, it is said that the Lion will always advance in life because his ruler never retrogrades.* – Witches All					

The Buzz from Beekeepers

WE LIVED for honey. We swallowed a spoonful in the morning to wake us up and one at night to put us to sleep. We took it with every meal to calm the mind, give us stamina, and prevent fatal disease. We swabbed ourselves in it to disinfect cuts or heal chapped lips. It went into our baths, our skin cream, our raspberry tea and biscuits. Nothing was safe from honey. In one week my skinny arms and legs began to plump out and the frizz in my hair turned to silken waves. August said that honey was the ambrosia of the gods and the shampoo of the goddesses.

– SUE MONK KIDD, *The Secret Life of Bees*

virgo

August 23 – September 22

Mutable Sign of Earth ♍ Ruled by Mercury ☿

VIRGO

S	M	T	W	T	F	S
BEES	AUG. 23	24 Barley Moon — Pisces	25 WANING	26	27 — Aries	28 Release old habits
29	30 Carry a wishing stone — Taurus	31 Raymond Buckland born, 1934	SEPT. 1 — Gemini	2	3 Speak of love — Cancer	4
5 — Leo	6 Jane Addams born, 1860	7 Tame the garden — Virgo	8	9 WAXING — Libra	10 Gather grains	11 Ganesh Festival — Scorpio
12	13 — Sagittarius	14	15	16 Do not babble — Capricorn	17 Weave a basket	18 — Aquarius
19 Whisper to Demeter	20	21 — Pisces	22 Plant bulbs			

Dawnsio, dawnsio, little bees –
keep to your hives and do not roam.

— from a Witch's blessing for honey

43

Creature Kinship

If you really understand an animal so that he gets to trust you completely and, within his limits, understands you, there grows up between you affection of a purity and simplicity which seems to me peculiarly satisfactory. There is also a cosmic strangeness about animals which always fascinates me and gives to my affection for them a mysterious depth or background.

— LEONARD WOOLF

libra

September 23 – October 22
Cardinal Sign of Air ♎ Ruled by Venus ♀

LIBRA

S	M	T	W	T	F	S
Venus' attributes were the swan, the dove and the pomegranate. — Greek Gods in Love				**SEPT. 23** Harvest Moon — Aries	**24** Autumnal Equinox ⇦	**25** WANING — Taurus
26	**27** Dine with a past love	**28** Gemini	**29** Lech Walesa born, 1943	**30** Cancer	**OCT. 1**	**2** Kiss the stars — Leo
3 Favor a cat	**4**	**5** Virgo	**6** Wash window sills	**7** Libra	**8** WAXING	**9** Scorpio
10	**11** Sagittarius	**12**	**13** Capricorn	**14**	**15** Perform a love spell	**16** Aquarius
17 Tell ghost stories	**18** Pisces	**19** Beware of a wolf's howl	**20** Bela Lugosi born, 1882	**21** Carry acorns for power — Aries	**22** Blood Moon	∂ o v e s

Eros always had his bow at the ready and his quiver contained two kinds of arrows: one is golden with dove feathers, the arrows invoking love at first sight; other arrows are leaden, fashioned with owl feathers, creating an indifferent lover.

— Greek Gods in Love

🦅 Maskers at Carnival, Alexandria 🦅

THE MADDEST aberrations of the city now come boldly forward under the protection of the invisible lords of Misrule who preside at this season. No sooner has darkness fallen than the maskers begin to appear in the streets – first in ones and twos then in small companies, often with musical instruments or drums, laughing and singing their way to some great houses or some night clubs where already the frosty air is bathed in the warmth of jazz – the cloying grunting intercourse of saxophones and drums. Everywhere they spring up in the pale moonlight, cowled like monks. The disguise gives them all a gloomy fanatical uniformity of outline which startles the white-robed Egyptians and fills them with alarm – the thrill of a fear which spices the wild laughter pouring out of the houses, carried by the light offshore winds toward the cafés on the sea front; a gaiety which by its very shrillness seems to tremble always upon the edge of madness.

Slowly the bluish spring moon climbs the houses, sliding up the minarets into the clicking palm trees, and with it the city seems to uncurl like some hibernating animal dug out of its winter earth, to stretch and begin to drink in the music of the three-day festival.

– *Lawrence Durrell*,
Alexandria Quartet, Balthazar

Celebrants male and female wear the domino (Latin, dominus, Lord) – a voluminous black hooded cape with an eye mask completely concealing gender and identity. A costume with infinite possibilities of mischief not lost on the author of these superb books.

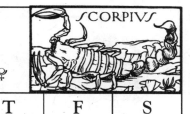

scorpio
October 23 – November 21
Fixed Sign of Water ▽ Ruled by Pluto ♀

S	M	T	W	T	F	S

phoenix

Some ancient myths tell us that the bird was crimson and gold and resembled an eagle; other legends claim that it was purple and resembled a heron; all agree that it was a creature of unsurpassed beauty.

– Magical Creatures

						Oct. 23 WANING Taurus
24	25 Richard E. Byrd born, 1888 Gemini	26	27 Burn mugwort	28 Clean mirrors Cancer	29	30 ◖ Leo
31 Samhain Eve	Nov. 1 Hallowmas Virgo	2 Visit ancestors' graves	3 Gather colorful leaves Libra	4	5 Remember fond times Scorpio	6 ●
7 Daylight Savings Time ends @ 2am Sagittarius	8 WAXING	9 Capricorn	10	11 Muse over old photos	12 Aquarius	13 ◗
14 Avoid conflict	15 Pisces	16 Hecate Night	17 Sprinkle salt about Aries	18	19 Make a recipe book Taurus	20 Robert F. Kennedy born, 1925
21 ◯ Snow Moon						

Alchemists chose the phoenix as their symbol and early chemists were located by the sign of the phoenix swinging above the door.

– Magical Creatures

47

Notable Quotations
ANIMALS

We need another and a wiser and perhaps a more mystical concept of animals… In a world older and more complete than ours they move finished and complete, gifted with extensions of the senses we have lost or never attained, living by voices we shall never hear. They are not brethren, they are not underlings; they are other nations, caught with ourselves in the net of life and time, fellow prisoners of the splendour and travail of the earth.

– Henry Beston

Dogs look up to us. Cats look down on us. Pigs treat us as equals.

–Winston Churchill

Don't approach a goat from the front, a horse from the back, or a fool from any side.

– Yiddish proverb

The bee is more honored than other animals, not because she labors, but because she labors for others.

– Saint John Chrysostom

I once had a sparrow alight upon my shoulder for a moment, while I was hoeing in a village garden, and I felt that I was more distinguished by that circumstance than I should have been by any epaulet I could have worn.

– Henry David Thoreau

There are two means of refuge from the miseries of life: music and cats.

– Albert Schweitzer

Our task must be to free ourselves… by widening our circle of compassion to embrace all living creatures and the whole of nature and its beauty.

– Albert Einstein

Any glimpse into the life of an animal quickens our own and makes it so much the larger and better in every way.

– John Muir

sagittarius
November 22 – December 20
Mutable Sign of Fire △ Ruled by Jupiter ♃

S	M	T	W	T	F	S
	Nov. 22 WANING Gemini	23	24 H. Toulouse-Lautrec born, 1864 Cancer	25 Cook with apples	26 Leo	27 Read Roman myths
28 ◐ Virgo	29	30	Dec. 1 Light candles Libra	2	3 Dream deeply Scorpio	4
5 ● Sagittarius	6 WAXING	7 Jack Frost visits Capricorn	8	9 Gaze at stars Aquarius	10	11
12 Pisces	13 ◑	14 Aries	15 Nero Caesar born, 0037	16 Fairy Queen Eve	17 Saturnalia Taurus	18 Bless the earth
19 Gemini	20 Watch snow fall					

CENTAUR

Man from head to torso, horse from torso south, centaurs canter along in the retinue of Dionysus, celebrating the rites and delights of the vine with Pan, Silenus, Eros, satyrs, nymphs and bacchantes. Like other rural divinities centaurs are gross brutes, prone to lechery and drunkenness…The exception was Chiron, educated by Apollo and Artemis, granted wisdom and eternal life.

– Magical Creatures

❧ Goats Nibble on Trees ❧

In a play of the fifth century B.C.E., a chorus of goats boasts of its appetite:

On arbutus, oak, and fir we feed, all sorts and conditions of trees,
Nibbling off the soft young green of these, and of these, and of these;
Olives tame and olives wild are theirs and thine and mine
Cytisus, maṣtich, salvia sweet and many-leaved eglantine,
Ivy and holm-oak, poplar and ash, buckthorn, willow and heather,
Asphodel, mullein, cistus, thyme and savory all together.
                                    – *Eupolis* (tr. Edmonds)

capricorn

December 21 – January 19
Cardinal Sign of Earth ♍ Ruled by Saturn ♄

S	M	T	W	T	F	S
Total lunar eclipse ⇨		DEC. **21** Oak Moon	**22** Winter Solstice ⇦ Cancer	**23** WANING	**24** Mark Prophet born, 1918 Leo	**25**
26 Watch sunrise Virgo	**27** Save pennies	**28** Libra	**29**	**30** Scorpio	**31** Wrap in a red blanket	JAN. **1** 2011 Sagittarius
2	**3** Partial solar eclipse ⇨ Capricorn	**4**	**5** WAXING	**6** Climb a hill Aquarius	**7** Polish copper	**8** Pisces
9 Feast of Janus	**10** Aries	**11** John Gadbury born, 1628	**12**	**13** Taurus	**14** Wish for a love	**15**
16 Gemini	**17** Whistle up a wind	**18** Bake bread Cancer	**19** Wolf Moon	GOAT		

Northern Europeans revered the nimble goat for its playful nature. The love goddess of Germanic tribes rode a goat to May Eve revels. Thor, Norse god of thunder, drove a chariot drawn by two fierce, unruly goats.

– Magical Creatures

Man of Signs

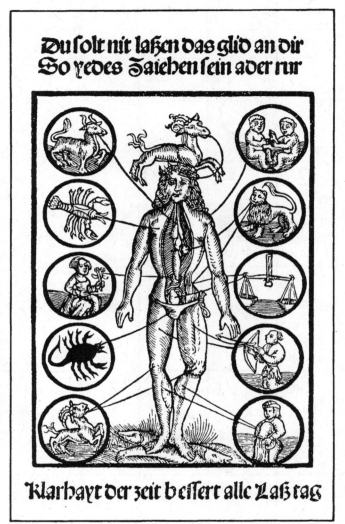

Du solt nit laßen das glid an dir
So yedes Zaichen sein ader rur

Klarhayt der zeit beffert alle Laß tag

Homo Signorum   Medieval Woodcut

Drawing blood was an ancient medical practice for the relief of ailments, sometimes with surgery, sometimes with leeches. In the old-dialect German of the chart, body parts suffering the bloodletting process were linked to the time of their astrological counterparts. According to the top line, "You should not let blood from any member of yours when the sign touches the proper vein." The lower line further cautions, "Clarity of the time improves every blood-letting day."

aquarius
January 20 – February 18
Fixed Sign of Air ♒ Ruled by Uranus ♅

S	M	T	W	T	F	S
SWAN	A Native American legend of the Blackfoot tribe depicts swans as helpers in a hero's quest to visit the sun. — *Magical Creatures*			Jan. **20** Linda Howe born, 1942 Leo	**21**	**22** Keep warm Virgo
23	**24** Draw flowers Libra	**25**	**26** Scorpio	**27**	**28** Sit by the fire Sagittarius	**29**
30	**31** Pour water from hand to earth Capricorn	Feb. **1** Oimelc Eve	**2** Year of the Rabbit Aquarius	**3** WAXING Candlemas ⇦	**4** Gaze into a crystal ball Pisces	**5**
6 The enlightened shine	**7** Charles Dickens born, 1812 Aries	**8**	**9** Avoid stubbornness Taurus	**10**	**11**	**12** Gemini
13	**14** Cancer	**15** Lupercalia	**16** Listen to sparrows sing Leo	**17**	**18** Storm Moon	S W A N

Apollo, Greek god of music and poetry, was linked to the bird, for it was believed that his soul passed into a swan. From this legend arose the tradition that the souls of all good poets live on as swans. Ben Jonson called Shakespeare the "Swan of Avon."
— *Magical Creatures*

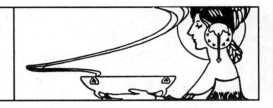

GARLIC
Ward off blandness

THE invaluable little bulb sheathed in its white jacket has an uncanny ability to change its nature. Pungent in a raw state, when cooked garlic surges to a sweetly mellow mood. Size also matters; the more it is minced, the stronger the flavor. But the cook needs to be wary of overcooking, especially in sautéing – burned garlic has a bitter flavor that will permeate the dish.

Roasting garlic is one of the simplest ways to enjoy the unique herb. Great as a spread for baguettes, vegetables, party dip or what you will, including the unusual chickpea salad below. To counteract the lingering odor of garlic once the dishes are enjoyed, follow by chewing parsley, mint or perhaps the most effective remedy – remove the white shell of cardamom and munch the fragrant black inner seed (do not swallow).

Roast Garlic

Peel away the outer layers of the bulb, leaving the skins of the cloves intact. Cut off the 1/4-inch to 1/2-inch tops of the cloves, exposing the cloves. Place the bulb in a pan and drizzle with about 1 tablespoon olive oil. Cover with aluminum foil and roast in a 400 degree F. oven for 30 minutes, or until the cloves are soft. Cool the garlic and press the root of the bulb to pop out the cloves.

Portuguese Chickpea and Roasted Garlic Salad

2 15-ounce cans chickpeas, drained
1 tablespoon fresh basil, chopped
2 tablespoons balsamic vinegar
1 bulb roast garlic cloves, recipe above
3 tomatoes, chopped
1 teaspoon ground cumin
salt, pepper

In a salad bowl mix chickpeas, basil and vinegar. Add roast garlic cloves, stirring well to coat the chickpeas. Add remaining ingredients, mix well and serve at room temperature. Serves 6.

For a delectable over-the-top garlic recipe (and nutritionist's nightmare), see Chicken with Forty Cloves of Garlic from Ina Garten's Barefoot Contessa in Paris *cookbook at www.TheWitchesAlmanac.com/AlmanacExtras.*

pisces
February 19 – March 20
Mutable Sign of Water ▽ Ruled by Neptune Ψ

S	M	T	W	T	F	S

 Hazelwood trees surrounded the Well of Wisdom. Nine nuts fell into the well. A salmon swallowed the hazelnuts and transformed into the Salmon of Wisdom, gaining all the knowledge in the world. That is how a magical fish swam into Celtic mythology!
— Barbara Stacy

FEB. 19
WANING
Virgo

20	21	22	23	24	25	26
Sidney Poitier born, 1927		Acquire a rose	Discard the unwanted	◐		
	Libra		Scorpio		Sagittarius	

27	28	MARCH 1	2	3	4	5
		Matronalia		Record dreams	●	Visions in a pool of water
Capricorn		Aquarius			Pisces	WAXING

6	7	8	9	10	11	12
	Love with passion	Luther Burbank born, 1849		Build a friendship		◑
Aries			Taurus		Gemini	

13	14	15	16	17	18	19
Daylight Savings Time begins @ 2am	Use good judgement in the home		Rescue a cat		Minerva's Day ⇨	◯ Chaste Moon
	Cancer		Leo		Virgo	

20
WANING

Finn MacCool, apprentice to a Druid, was given the captured Salmon of Wisdom to cook. He burned his thumb and sucked the blister, transferring the wisdom. Finn MacCool became a great Irish hero, summoning powers whenever he sucked his thumb.
— Barbara Stacy

SALMON OF WISDOM

The Man in Black

Discourse with the Devil?

AT THE TRIAL of Bideford witches in North Devonshire, 1682, Susanna Edwards said she had been gathering firewood in a field when she met a gentleman all dressed in black. She begged some money from him and "the man in black" said that if she granted him any request she would nevermore lack meat, drink and clothes. He then vanished and she realized he was the Devil. Another defendant, Temperance Lloyd, was accused of using the magical art, sorcery and witchcraft for harm and having "discourse or familiarity with the Devil."

Nearly 250 years later, in 1928, it was reported that in Cambridgeshire a witch called Old Mother Redcap (a generic title for female witches) had been visited by the Devil. He appeared at her door with a book and asked her to sign it. In return he gave her five familiars in the shape of a rat, a cat, a toad, a ferret and a mouse. Their names were Bonnie, Blue Cap, Red Cap, Jupiter, and Venus. In one version of the story, Mother Redcap inherited her powers from another famous witch, Daddy Heath, who lived in a nearby village. When she died, the "man in black" delivered a box to her successor containing the five familiars.

Who was this mysterious figure known as "the Man in Black"? Both the witch hunters and the accused believed that he was the Devil himself. Accounts of his vanishing into thin air and walking through walls or locked doors to manifest to his followers in prison cells would seem to confirm he was a supernatural entity.

Magic or mask?

Before the publication of Dr. Margaret Murray's books, *The Witch Cult in Western Europe* (1921) and *The God of the Witches* (1931), those who believed in the reality of witchcraft accepted the orthodox Christian view that the male deity worshipped by the witches was His Satanic Majesty.

Doctor Murray put forward the alternative that the medieval witch cult was the survival of a prehistoric fertility religion and the "man in black" described as the Devil was in fact a pre-Christian horned god.

However, Doctor Murray went even further than that as she claimed that the "Devil" who presided over the Witches' Sabbath was in fact a human being who sometimes appeared in the costume of the time or disguised in a mask, as at North Berwick. Historical witches said that the Devil appeared at the Sabbath in different animal forms. These included a bull, ram, goat, stag and a black dog. Doctor Murray's theory was that this was the male leader of the witches' coven wearing an animal skin and mask or head. Witches often said that their Dark Master's voice was gruff, deep or harsh and Doctor Murray said this suggested he was speaking from behind a mask.

The Magister factor

The late Cecil Williamson, founder of the witchcraft museums at Castletown on the Isle of Man and Boscastle in Cornwall, told the writer that the concept of the "Man in Black" was adopted by the Walsingham Craft in the late sixteenth century. This witch tradition was named after Sir Francis Walsingham, the confidant of Queen Elizabeth I and founder of the British Secret Service.

Sir Francis recruited witches to form a network of spies and undercover agents to report back to him about the activities of England's enemies. The "Man in Black" was the title for a local leader of the witch cult who supervised several covens or solitary witches in an area.

Today in modern traditional witchcraft the term "Man in Black" is sometimes used for the Magister (Master) of a "covine" or the leader of a tradition. Some traditional witches, such as Robert Cochrane, also resurrected the archaic title of "Devil" for the leader. As in the Walsingham Craft, it is also used to describe a Magister who rules several covines.

The nineteenth-century English "cunning man" or wizard George Pickingill took this role, as he was a "master of witches." It is said that if he stood at his cottage door and blew three times on a wooden whistle, all the witches in the village were forced to appear at the site and reveal themselves.

– MICHAEL HOWARD

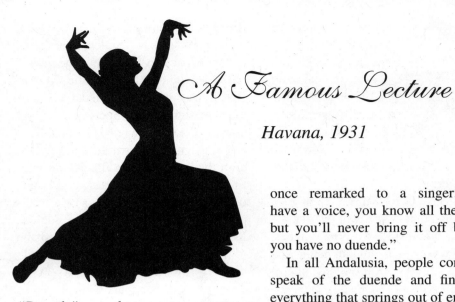

A Famous Lecture

Havana, 1931

"Duende" may be a new concept to some readers, as it is a new concept to the English language. The latest edition of The Random House Dictionary *uneasily defines the word for the first time: "1. A goblin, demon, spirit; 2. Inspiration, magic, fire." The principle is elusive, but duende was best illuminated by the great Andalusian poet and playwright, Federico Garcia Lorca, in a famous lecture. Lorca captured the spirit of duende in this address, performed in Havana in 1931 and excerpted below. His superb poetry and the play "Blood Wedding," among others, are afire with dark magic. Considered the greatest Spanish poet of the century, Lorca's life was cut short by bullets in the Granada night by Fascists during the Spanish Civil War. He was thirty-eight years old.*

Federico Garcia Lorca's utterance illuminates duende:

"NOW THAT has real duende!" It was in this spirit that Manuel Torres, the great artist of the Andalusian people, once remarked to a singer: "You have a voice, you know all the styles, but you'll never bring it off because you have no duende."

In all Andalusia, people constantly speak of the duende and find it in everything that springs out of energetic instinct. That marvelous singer, "El Librijano," observed, "Whenever I am singing with duende, no one can come up to me"; and one day the old gypsy dancer, "La Malena," exclaimed while listening to Brailowski play a fragment of Bach: "Olé! That has duende !" – and remained bored by Gluck and Brahms and Darius Milhaud. And Manuel Torres once uttered this splendid phrase while listening to Falla himself play his "Nocturno del Generalife": "Whatever has black sounds has duende." There is no greater truth.

These black sounds are the mystery, the roots that probe through the mire that we all know of, and do not understand, but which furnishes us with whatever is sustaining in art. Black sounds: so said the celebrated Spaniard, thereby concurring with Goethe, who, in effect, defined the duende when he said, speaking of Paganini: "A mysterious power that all may feel and no philosophy can explain."

The duende, then, is a power and not a construct, is a struggle and not a concept. I have heard an old guitarist, a true virtuoso, remark, "The duende is not in the throat, the duende comes up from inside, up from the very soles of the feet." That is to say, it is not a question of aptitude, but of a true and viable style of blood, in other words; of what is oldest in culture: of creation made act.

The Poets of the Muse hear voices and do not know where they come from; but surely they are from the Muse, who encourages and at times devours them entirely. The Muse arouses the intellect, bearing landscapes of columns and the false taste of laurel; but intellect is oftentimes the foe of poetry because it imitates too much, it elevates the poet to a throne of acute angles and makes him forget that in time the ants can devour him.

The true struggle is with the Duende. To seek out the Duende, however, neither map nor discipline is required. Enough to know that he kindles the blood like an irritant, that he exhausts, that he repulses all the bland geometrical assurances, that he smashes the styles.

The great artists of southern Spain, both gypsies and flamenco, whether singing or dancing or playing their instruments, know that no emotion is possible without the mediation of the Duende. They may hoodwink the people, they may give the illusion of duende without really having it, just as writers and painters and literary fashion mongers without duende cheat you daily; but it needs only a little care and the will to resist one's own indifference, to discover the imposture and put it and its crude artifice to flight.

The arrival of the Duende always presupposes a radical change in all the forms as they existed on the old plane. It gives a sense of refreshment unknown until then, together with that quality of the just opening rose, of the miraculous, which comes and instills an almost religious transport.

In all Arabian music, in the dances, songs, elegies of Arabia, the coming of the Duende is greeted by fervent outcries of Allah! Allah! God! God!, so close to the Olé! Olé! of our bull rings that who is to say they are not actually the same; and in all the songs of southern Spain the appearance of the duende is followed by heartfelt exclamations of God alive! profound, human tender, the cry of communion with God through the medium of the five senses and the grace of the Duende that stirs the voice and the body of the dancer – a flight from this world, both real and poetic

Naturally, when flight is achieved, all feel its effects: the initiate coming to see at last how style triumphs over inferior matter, and the unenlightened, through

the I don't know what of an authentic emotion. Some years ago, in a dancing contest at Jerez de la Frontera, an old lady of eighty, competing against beautiful women and young girls with waists as supple as water, carried off the prize merely by the act of raising her arms, throwing back her head, and stamping the little platform with a blow of her feet; but in the conclave of muses and angels foregathered there – beauties of form and beauties of smile – the dying duende triumphed as it had to, trailing the rusted knife blades of its wings along the ground.

All the arts are capable of duende, but it naturally achieves its widest play in the fields of music, dance and the spoken poem, since those require a living presence to interpret them, because they are forms which grow and decline perpetually and raise their contours on the precise present.

Often the Duende of the musician passes over into the Duende of the interpreter, and at other times, when the musician and poet are not matched, the duende of the interpreter this is interesting creates a new marvel that retains the appearance and the appearance only of the originating form. Such was the case with the duende ridden Duse who deliberately sought out failures in order to turn them into triumphs, thanks to her capacity for invention; or with Paganini who, as Goethe explained, could make one hear profoundest melody in out and out vulgarity; or with a delectable young lady from the port of Santa María whom I saw singing and dancing the horrendous Italian ditty, "O Marie!" with such rhythms, such pauses, and such conviction that she transformed an Italian gee-gaw into a hard serpent of raised gold. What happened, in effect, was that each in his own way found something new, something never before encountered, which put lifeblood and art into bodies void of expression.

This is interesting and must be underscored. The Duende never repeats himself, any more than the forms of the sea repeat themselves in a storm.

– FEDERICO GARCIA LORCA
The Play and Theory of Duende, 1930

For fine examples of duende in poetry, give yourself the pleasure of Lorca and his peers at our website, www.The WitchesAlmanac.com/AlmanacExtras.

Window on the Weather

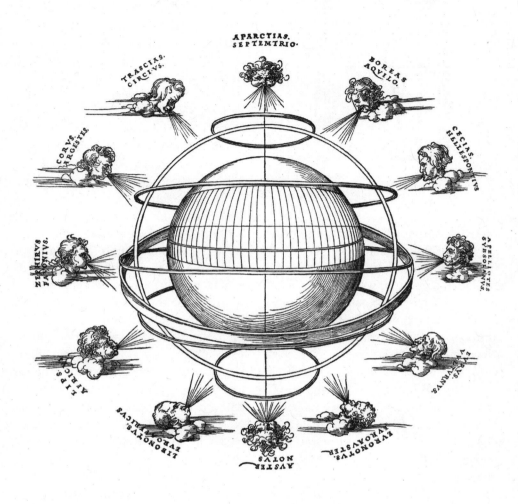

The weather-cock on the church spire, though made of iron, would soon be broken by the storm-wind if it did not understand the noble art of turning to every wind.

— HEINRICH HEINE

SPRING

MARCH 2010. The remnants of a weak El Niño weather pattern will likely bring an early start to the tornado season in the South, with the Southeast and Gulf Coast especially vulnerable. Late winter snowfall will be heavy across the Great Lakes, the Rockies and New England, after a winter of record cold. Storms will be long lasting in the Northeast, as storms stall in the ocean bringing abundant Atlantic moisture inland. This year's snow cover will be unusually long lasting, similar to the winter of 2002/2003 when similar solar and ocean water conditions occurred. Energy demand should last well into the spring this year. West Coast rainfall will be plentiful, easing critical water shortages in Southern California.

APRIL 2010. Rainfall amounts will be closely monitored again this spring, in the wake of last year's Midwest flooding. A late planting season is possible again, as the pattern still favors above-normal rain and below-normal temperatures. Sunshine will be limited in the Northeast, where sprawling ocean storms will bring a gray sky, dense coastal fog and bouts of rain and wet snow across the interior. In Florida, conditions remain wet and the threat of fire will be minimal. Tornadoes remain a concern for a few communities near the Gulf Coast and Mississippi Valley. Several strong West Coast storms will bring high winds and heavy rain to the region.

MAY 2010. Remnants from last year's El Niño Pacific Ocean phenomena will impact this year's spring weather. Rainfall will be heavy across the South, with a continued high frequency of severe weather, including the risk of tornadoes. In general, temperatures will be below normal there, with limited sunshine. Farther north, days of 70 degree warmth will be infrequent from Chicago to Minneapolis. Combined with above-normal rainfall, the spring planting season will be delayed by the threat of frost. In the Northeast, a day of record-breaking heat will be followed by several long spells of wet and cool weather. On the West Coast, spring storms will ease and tranquil weather will persist through much of the month.

SUMMER

JUNE 2010. Across the eastern half of the nation, sunshine will shine below its potential this month. Southern rains will be heavy and northern jet stream energy will carry moisture northward, keeping the Midwest and New England wet and cool. Several days of rain will be followed by brief sunny spells. This was a common theme last summer and the higher forces that caused this pattern are still in place. Some cities will likely report record cool. In the Southern Plains, temperatures will be hot and the air dry. The West Coast will experience cool and steady ocean breezes with rare rainfall in Southern California.

JULY 2010. From Washington D.C. to New England and westward to Chicago, summer heat will be short lived. Normal high temperatures in the 80s will be reached for only several days. However, sunshine will be prevalent, even as spells of gusty thunderstorms sweep through many communities during the afternoon and evenings.

Rainfall will be especially heavy from the mid-Atlantic to New England and the Central Ohio Valley. A rare summer cold front will breeze through northern Florida, bringing brief relief from summer heat. Monsoon rains will be heavy this year in the Southwest. Thunderstorms will clip the northern Rockies in Montana and Idaho.

AUGUST 2010. Cooler Atlantic Ocean water temperatures that began during the last eight years will subdue hurricane activity there for years to come. A greater frequency of these storms will occur in the Pacific, though few will threaten land. Seasonably cool weather will cover the East this month, though tinges of fall foliage will be seen in Northern New England and the Rockies by the twentieth. This will result from less summer sunshine than usual, happening from above-normal rainfall. Temperatures will continue below normal in both locations with the Southern Plains experiencing intense heat. California will experience hot and dry weather, though reservoirs will remain high from the abundant rainfall of the previous winter.

AUTUMN

SEPTEMBER 2010. Any Atlantic hurricanes will be confined to mid month. At most one storm will be severe and likely stay at sea. Low sunspot activity and two recent volcanoes will keep temperatures cool across much of the country and an early frost can easily occur anywhere in the Northeast and Great Lakes by the end of the month. Normal rainfall amounts can be expected, though few of the usual evening showers that occur in the southern Appalachians will occur. Florida's West Coast thunderstorm season will ease early this year and autumn fires will threaten Southern California. A brief snowfall will dust the Colorado Rockies around the 20th.

OCTOBER 2010. Fall color will arrive quickly, first along the Canadian border and arriving in North Georgia by the 20th. The growing season will end with an early frost in New England and the Northern Plains. Remnants from last year's chilly pattern will bring snow to the Southern and Central Rockies, as the Aspens turn golden yellow. Much of the country will be dry; especially in Florida fires in the Everglades can occur. West Coast weather is mild from Central California to Seattle, while fires still threaten Southern California. A late-season hurricane will roam the Gulf of Mexico waters and may threaten the Florida Keys.

NOVEMBER 2010. Pleasantly cool and dry weather will begin the month in the Southeast. Cool weather will be firmly established in Florida, with pleasantly warm days and comfortably cool nights. While fair weather will dominate the Northeast, temperatures will average below normal and mountain snow flurries will cover New Hampshire's White Mountains by the fifteenth. The snowpack will quickly build in the Rockies from New Mexico to Wyoming. Rain arrives in Central and Southern California, reducing the fire danger. The Southern Plains are dry and unseasonably warm, while early season lake effect snowfall is likely near the Great Lakes by the twentieth.

WINTER

DECEMBER 2010. A general snow-cover forms quickly from Southern Pennsylvania and through the lack of sunspot activity favors an early winter. In fact, it was during a similar pattern that George Washington crossed the Delaware River in the late 1700s; a time that marked the beginning of a brutal cold winter. Snow will also fall early across the Midwest and Great Plains. North winds will change a cold rain to ice in Dallas and a brief snowfall can also occur in such Southwest cities as Las Vegas and Albuquerque. West Coast storms shift south and end the fire season. Mountain snow is heavy in the peaks surrounding Los Angeles.

JANUARY 2011. Though last year's all-time record cold, set in Maine and Illinois, may not be reached, below-normal temperatures can be expected once again. In fact, low sunspot activity that began a decade ago will persist and continue a shift to cooler temperatures. Several freezes are possible in Florida this year as Arctic air spreads south. As many as three coastal storms will form with great suddenness and bring snow and wind from Washington D.C. to Portland, Maine. Snowfall will occur frequently in California, Sierra Nevada. Bitter cold and dry weather will cover the nation's heartland.

FEBRUARY 2011. The worst of the Eastern cold will ease by mid month; the normal course for winter temperatures. Snowfall is destined to remain above normal and cover much of the East, Midwest and Southern Plains. Snowfall will remain heavy in California's mountains and fall again in the Colorado Rockies. Several strong storms will strike Central California with gale force winds. In fact, snow can fall in the hills of the South Bay. Below-zero cold will be felt early in the month in the Northern Plains and New England.

The Magic of O

A contemporary symbol for change

LOGOS AND SYMBOLS have played meaningful roles in the world of the mystic since earliest times. Powerful images speak to the deepest realms of the subconscious and convey significant messages at a glance. Some spiritual and religious emblems as well as marketing and political icons survive for many years, sometimes for centuries. Protection, success and other qualities are assigned to cherished symbols which can be used as ritual jewelry or to create sacred space. Other designs evoke little reaction and eventually disappear, growing obscure along with their original ideas or personality associations.

Barack Obama's distinctive O logo became familiar during the memorable and volatile presidential campaign of 2008. Obama claimed the initial O much as George W. Bush had claimed the W years earlier. The Obama symbol begins with a blue circle as a background and red stripes to honor the stars-and-stripes colors of the American flag. Three red stripes flowing diagonally across the bottom of the circle relate to the plains and farmland, while a second white circle inside the blue field hints at a shining sunrise over the plains. Because the Sun is white, it does evoke a sunrise, not a sunset. The logo carries the message of a new morning Sun. It brings both hope and change as it rises over America, suggesting that Obama is it. Astrologers will notice that the Sun rules Leo, the birth sign of President Obama, who was born on August 4.

A deeper analysis of this important new symbol reveals that it suggests a Van Gogh painting, "The Sower," as well as a Thomas Hart Benton Depression-era farm scene. None of the other 2008 presidential candidates had logos comparable to this level of meaning.

The stylized eagle of Mitt Romney, Hillary Clinton's ribbon of stars and stripes, Mike Huckabee's yellow letters with flowing stars and stripes as a background, John Mc Cain's single military-badge star suspended against a black background – all are barely recollected. Each of these carried the name of the candidate, while Obama's illustrated only his initial. After the campaign an entire building, a small-town gas station, was painted to illustrate the Obama Sun. The beloved symbol appears often, becoming an ever-more familiar emblem of promise. During these times of growth and transition, we cling to the O motif on clothing, posters and publications as it works its magic to bring much needed hope and change.

The red, white and blue color combination in itself has long been fortunate. During World War II all of the victorious Allied Forces (the United States, Great Britain and France) had flags of red, white and blue. The chakra colors aligning the root or base of spine chakra, the throat and finally the crown are linked to the red, blue and white light, respectively.

Brilliantly created by Sol Sender of Sender LLC, a Chicago design firm (with input from his design team and the Obama campaign, Sender says), the radiant sun symbol does have its detractors. Some have called it a prophecy for the sunset of an empire. Others see in it an insulting parody of the familiar sun at the center of Japan's flag. Ultimately only time will tell what the symbol will mean. However its magic is powerful and universal at present. The symbol is a true "sign of the times." Focus on it to enhance levels of comfort and encouragement to successfully meet contemporary challenges.

– ESTHER NEUMEIER

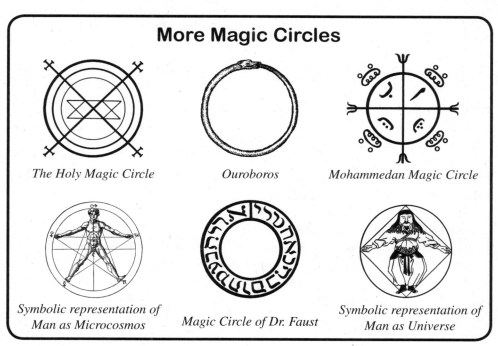

More Magic Circles

The Holy Magic Circle

Ouroboros

Mohammedan Magic Circle

Symbolic representation of Man as Microcosmos

Magic Circle of Dr. Faust

Symbolic representation of Man as Universe

Prospero

All hail, great master

PROSPERO IS THE greatest sorcerer who never lived, dazzling us with magical art springing from the brain of another sorcerer. Shakespeare weaves his incomparable spell in *The Tempest* and furnishes Prospero with powers undreamed of by the most skilled mortal practitioners. And so we hail the fictional master, who through the course of the romantic drama creates "amazements" only a genius could conceive.

Primary, of course, is the tempest itself, the "wild waters in this roar" consuming the first scene which brings the magician's enemies to his disposal. Only Prospero has the mojo to conjure up such a violent storm, unless we look to Zeus the Thunderer. The Elizabethans, like the Greeks, dearly loved ferocity, and the terrified sailors assume they are dead men. The boatswain whimpers, "Must our mouths be cold?" No. Although he has caused the boat to smash, Prospero saves the sailors. And he draws to his enchanted isle the people aboard needed to accomplish his purposes.

His endeavor is dual, to exact revenge on his treacherous brother Antonio and to find a husband for his beautiful daughter. He and Miranda have been marooned on a desert island for thirteen years. As the Duke of Milan, Prospero neglected his realm to immerse himself in the study of magic, leaving his duties to Antonio. His brother usurps the duchy and casts Prospero and his child adrift in a decaying boat. Gonzalo, a loyal courtier, secretly provides them with "rich garments, linens, stuffs and necessaries," including the books that Prospero values above his dukedom. Father and daughter land on a mysterious desert island populated only by two inhuman entities.

Ariel is an air spirit who carries out Prospero's magic, and the master can make him perform unimaginable tasks. When Ariel is summoned he declares:

Grave sir, hail! I come
To answer thy best pleasure; be't to fly,
To swim, to dive into the fire, to ride
On the curl'd clouds; to thy strong
bidding task
Ariel and all his quality.

And Prospero confers a task beyond the skill of most magicians:

Go make thyself like a nymph o'
the sea: be subject
To no sight but thine and mine; invisible
To every eyeball else.

For a servant of the all-powerful Prospero, no sooner said than vanished.

Caliban, the other magical entity, is another story. The monstrous "thing most brutish" believes that he is the rightful ruler of the island. Caliban and Prospero are bitter enemies and Prospero imposes dire penalties for defiance:

For this, be sure, to-night thou
  shalt have cramps
Side-stitches that shall pen thy
  breast up; Urchins
Shall forth at vast of night that
  they may work
All exercise on thee: thou shalt
  be pinch'd
As thick as honeycomb,
  each pinch more stinging
As bees that made them.

To which Caliban growls, "Fill all thy bones with aches; make thee roar,/That beasts shall tremble at thy din."

The shipwrecked Ferdinand emerges, Prospero's bridegroom of choice for Miranda. Of course it is love at first sight for the handsome prince and Miranda and things are settled briskly:

Ferdinand: O you! So perfect
  and so peerless
Miranda: I would not wish any
  companion in the world but you.
Do you love me?
Ferdinand: I, beyond all limit of
  what else i' the world,
Do love, prize and honour you.

Miranda wastes no more time. "I am your wife, if you will marry me," Ferdinand vows eternal love, and Prospero sets them playing chess to keep the couple from carnal matters until after the wedding.

Complications abound, including a plot by Caliban to kill Prospero with the gruesome "knock of a nail in his head," fortunately prevented. The wizard turns his attention to completing revenge over his brother. Antonio and his companions wander the island in confusion and the invisible wizard hovers above them. Suddenly they are frightened to hear the "solemn and strange music" created by Prospero. The play is replete with the magic of music, affecting the heart of even the brutish Caliban:

Sometimes a thousand twanging
  instruments
Will hum about mine ears; and
  sometimes voices,
That, if I then had wak'd after
  long sleep,
Will make me sleep again; and
  then, in dreaming,
The clouds methought would open
  and show riches
Ready to drop upon me; that,
  when I wak'd,
I cried to dream again.

As the castaways marvel at the music, several strange Shapes enter, "bringing

in a banquet: they dance about it with gentle actions of salutation." And silently encouraging the guests to eat, they vanish. The shipwrecked group is stunned. What caused the "marvelous sweet music"? What were the "Shapes"? From where does the enchantment spring? One courtier declares, "A living drollery. Now I will believe/That there are unicorns." The banquet fare looks delicious, but they hesitate to taste the spooky food. Just as they decide to eat, they hear thunder and lightning. Ariel appears like a harpy, claps his wings and the viands vanish.

Now Prospero conjures up the most dazzling display from his bag of magic – the appearance of three goddesses to bless the love-dazed couple. Iris, the rainbow divinity, "watery arch and messenger," summons Ceres, goddess of grain. She promises:

Earth's increase, profuse plenty
Barns and garners never empty;
Vines with clust'ring bunches growing;
Plants with goodly burden bowing;
Scarcity and want shall shun you;
Ceres' blessing so is on you.

Now the queen of goddesses adds the
grace we would wish all lovers:
Honour, riches, marriage-blessing,
Long continuance and increasing,
Hourly joys be still upon you!
Juno sings her blessings on you!

Prospero forgives his enemies and prepares to forsake his enchanted isle. He must resume his responsibilities as the Duke of Milan, including a great wedding for Miranda and the prince. But in order to rejoin the world Prospero must be willing to "drown his books" and renounce his powers. Behind Prospero's words we hear the voice of his magical Elizabethan creator:

Our revels now are ended.
  These our actors,
As I foretold you, were all spirits and
Are melted into thin air;
And, like the baseless fabric
  of his vision,
The cloud-capped towers,
  the gorgeous palaces,
The solemn temples, the great
  Globe itself,
Yes, all which it inherit, shall dissolve,
And, like this insubstantial
  pageant faded
Leave not a rack behind.
  We are such stuff
As dreams are made on,
  and our little life
Is rounded with a sleep.

– BARBARA STACY

Hell-Broth

Hecate and the Weird Sisters
stir up a steaming pot of wickedness

Fillet of a fenny snake,
In the cauldron boil and bake;
Eye of newt and toe of frog,
Wool of bat and tongue of dog,
Adder's fork and blind worm's sting,
Lizard's leg and owlet's wing,
For a charm of powerful trouble,
Like a hell broth boil and bubble.
          – SHAKESPEARE, *Macbeth* (IV.i)

Markeb

Travels with a scholarly sailor

28 Degrees Virgo 54 minutes

THE POSITION of the stars has been used to track every moment of time since before 500 B.C.E. The Pentagon agrees with the astrological records, and the Department of Astronomy sends a courteous letter of verification upon request. The stellar bodies are divided into three groups. First and foremost are the luminaries, the two great lights of the Sun (greater luminary) and Moon (lesser luminary). Next consider the planets, those heavenly bodies which orbit the Sun along with the Earth. Planet actually means "wanderer." Finally there are the fixed stars. These twinkling night lights seem to be immovable. Eventually sky watchers realized the fixed stars do move, but very slowly in an immense, inconceivable orbit through deep space.

Each of the fixed stars is actually a sun, shining with its own light just like our own greater luminary. Size, distance and temperature are factors in the specific impacts of the various stars. They do have definite affects. The stars figure prominently in the interpretation of individual natal charts as well as in the astrology of world events.

The brightness of a star is called its magnitude, the level of power. The color shows the temperature, which in turn describes the exact nature of the celestial energy it offers. The vast distances separating the stars from each other, and from Earth, are barely comprehensible. To grasp them, we must think in light years. Light moves at 186,330 miles each single second. A light year is the actual distance that light travels in a calendar year. The closest stars are about four light years away. Others are more distant, at hundreds and even thousands of light years away. Still, a prominent fixed star in a birth chart can color an individual's entire life. A passing stellar influence, coming from an eclipse or combined with a planet's transit, shows a turning point affecting the entire planet. A very small orb of no more than 3 degrees is used in interpreting fixed stars. Most astrologers feel that they "cast no rays." This phrase means that the conjunction is the only aspect considered. In other cases, some astrologers argue that the opposition is also significant.

Markeb is a fixed star whose influence will be especially important this year. Currently located in Virgo at 28 degrees 54 minutes, its nature is a fortunate one, reflecting the higher attributes of both Jupiter and Saturn. Markeb will be emphasized by a conjunction with Saturn transiting Virgo and an opposition to both Jupiter and Uranus in Pisces. Allowing a 3 degree orb, Saturn will conjoin Markeb from early spring until the end of August. Jupiter will oppose this star from mid May through June and again during January. Uranus will be in orb by opposition all year. The Full Moon on March 19, 2011 is at 28 degrees Virgo 48 minutes, ending the winter with an almost exact conjunction to the star. This is an augury of profound importance.

Markeb (not to be confused with two malevolent stars called Markab and Menkar) appears as a small white light in the constellation Argus, The Ship. It relates to the acquisition of knowledge, pious faith in goodness, voyages, expansion and profit. There is a caution with virtuous Markeb. Keeping bad company, attempting indiscretions or illegal ventures will meet with disaster or even imprisonment. Acting with propriety, always with pure and positive intent, results in a positive pull from this star which straddles Virgo and Libra.

Birthdays from September 19th through the 24th are in conjunction with Markeb. In other horoscopes, consider planets located between 26 degrees of Virgo to 1 degree of Libra for the conjunction and 26 degrees of Pisces to 1 degree of Aries for the more subtle opposition.

– DIKKI-JO MULLEN

Keynotes for Markeb and the current 2010-2011 transits:

With Saturn: Legacies, intergenerational dynamics, quiet, thoughtful guidance
With Jupiter: Justice served, helping hand, travel, healing
With Uranus: New associates, politics, technology, metaphysics, applied astrology and progressive thought
With the Full Moon: Domestic gains, improvement in health care, new discoveries about plants and small animals, successful employment

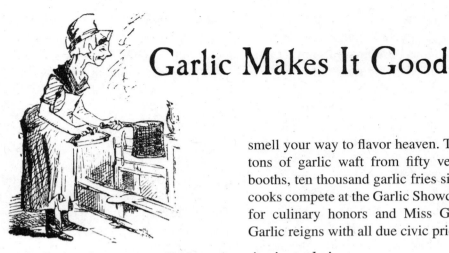

Garlic Makes It Good

GARLIC is the most affable of foods, treasured the world over for its incomparable character. Alice May Brock, author of *Alice's Restaurant Cookbook,* got it right: "Sour cream makes it Russian, lemon and cinnamon make it Greek, soy sauce makes it Chinese, garlic makes it good." The herb's pungent flavor adds character to all kinds of cookery, giving wake-up calls to soups and stews, roasts and sautéed dishes, whatever goes into a pan. In its raw state garlic adds legendary sass to salads.

Allium sativum is kin to other global members of the onion family, shallots, leeks and chives. The biggest annual crop (23 billion pounds) derives from China, followed by India, South Korea, Russia and the U.S. Most of the American yield comes from Gilroy, California, known enthusiastically if not accurately as "the garlic capital of the world." Every July for the past thirty years Gilroy has hosted a three-day Garlic Festival benefit and the town is awash in pungency. If you know the way to San Jose and can't locate nearby Gilroy, open your car windows and smell your way to flavor heaven. Three tons of garlic waft from fifty vendor booths, ten thousand garlic fries sizzle, cooks compete at the Garlic Showdown for culinary honors and Miss Gilroy Garlic reigns with all due civic pride.

Ancient admirers

Around five thousand years ago garlic made its virtues known to the world. The earliest Egyptians were obsessed with the herb, believing that it strengthened the body and fought off infection. Pyramid builders consumed garlic much as today's Andean farmers chew coca leaves, stimulants to keep on keeping on. The entire population enjoyed garlic, including the Pharaoh. Little garlic bulbs fashioned of clay accompanied King Tutankhamen in his tomb and garlic was so prized that it passed as currency. Early Greek and Roman soldiers received garlic before they engaged in battle, believing that the herb provided courage as well as stamina. Greek Olympic athletes, millennia removed from steroids, ate garlic to enhance their performances. The herb has been used for the same goal as an aphrodisiac. The Talmud tells followers that garlic warms the body, "makes the face shine," and increases seminal fluid. The Jewish scribe Ezra recommended that garlicky foods be eaten on Friday night, ritual time for marital lovemaking.

Sacramental services

The inhabitants of Pelusium in Lower Egypt considered it taboo to eat garlic,  for the plant itself was worshipped as a deity. Garlic was invoked by the ancient Egyptians before taking oaths, according to Pliny, the deification serving to solemnize the vow. But garlic also served as food for gods, especially for Hecate. The Greeks believed that the Goddess of the Crossroads enjoyed garlic for supper and so perhaps did her infamous baying hounds – garlic was left on piles of stones where three roads met. Taoist mythology evolved around black garlic, dried at length until the cloves turned the color of onyx and still available. Chewing six cloves, according to tradition, altered genetics and conferred immortality by strengthening the chi, the vital energy. Korean women with "bear or tiger temperaments" were encouraged by would-be spouses to eat the six black garlic cloves to achieve supernatural powers. According to folklore the herb repels the Evil Eye and drives off jealous nymphs said to envy pregnant women.

Garlic sometimes had a less idyllic occult role. According to one Christian belief, after Satan left the Garden of Eden garlic arose in his left footprint and onion in his right. Considering that the left side was "sinister" according to linguistic root (see the WA 2009/2010), the doctrine implied an evil food. Hindus refrain from using garlic in fare for religious festivals and events, Muslims consider it inappropriate to eat garlic before going to mosque, and Jains avoid eating garlic altogether.

Garlic is like six doctors

Fortunately there is no such thing as a cure-all or there would be standing room only on earth. But down through the ages people have attributed almost magical qualities to particular foods  or beverages, including a variety of teas, herbs and oils. Since antiquity garlic has been regarded as a remedy for a dizzying diversity of ailments. Some of the early prescriptions worked effectively, others were fanciful.

In Egypt garlic was standard treatment for wounds, infections, tumors, heart disease, lack of stamina and intestinal parasites. Ancient Greeks and Romans used it for some of the above as well as asthma, leprosy, bladder infections and repelling scorpions. African farmers chewed the herb in the fields, believing that it relieved them from the hot sun. Garlic has a long history as a remedy for hoarseness, and the Cherokee used it for coughs and croup. Early Persians must have been enthusiastic consumers; an early tablet records a grocer's order for 395,000 bulbs.

The Dracula factor

Garlic is famous for repelling the chi-i-i-ildren of the ni-i-ight, thanks to author Bram Stoker and the spooky Transylvanian accent of Bela Lugosi, the original screen Dracula. Garlic could do the job by being worn, hung from doors or windows, rubbed on chimneys or keyholes. Beyond the Stoker/Rice vampire connection lurks a real element – the ability of garlic to "ward off" or repel what is malignant. Modern scientists have learned that garlic has certain properties that may be considered antibacterial, antiviral, anti-inflammatory and antibiotic, effective as remedies as well as preventives.

During the Middle Ages garlic was thought to be an antidote for the plague sweeping Europe and patients were dosed with the herb. As double protection braids of bulbs hung across doorways to prevent entrance to evil spirits inciting the disease. The seventeenth century English physician Nicholas Culpeper credits garlic with healing the bites of mad dogs, ridding children of worms and cleaning up acne. In 1858 the French microbiologist Louis Pasteur came up with the earliest modern experiment. He placed the cloves in a petri dish filled with bacteria and noticed a few days later that each clove occupied a bacteria-free area. Thanks to Pasteur garlic was taken seriously as an antiseptic, especially in wartime, when medical supplies were unavailable. During World War I, British doctors used garlic as a remedy for gangrene and mixed the herb's juice with peat moss to bandage wounds. Russian physicians did the same during WWII and also fed the troops with garlic to prevent disease, so much that garlic was termed "Russian penicillin."

The familiar downside
From the time of the ancient Greeks and Romans garlic has been known as "the stinking rose." The reason for "stinking" is obvious but the rose connection is mysterious – no botanical link exists nor does garlic look particularly like that flower. The oddity is that garlic smells delicious as it cooks but leaves a rather disagreeable odor from the mouth and pores. If garlic may serve as an aphrodisiac, its odor may ward off, perhaps a neutral situation.

For the sake of flavor the downside has long been tolerated in Mediterranean Europe, but garlic was a rarity in English and American cuisines. The herb was considered "ethnic," sometimes a buzzword for disdainful class attitude. But the last half century has seen immense food changes in both countries, and garlic enjoys widespread enthusiasm as these cuisines become ever more adventurous and chefs become superstars. Queen Elizabeth II and Prince Philip may be the last holdouts. When the couple visited the Quirinale Palace in Rome a few years ago, apparently they feared that exuberant Italian chefs might actually get giddy with garlic. Chefs were instructed to keep the royal menus garlic free. Heaven only knows what consternation that might have caused in the *cucina* awash in garlic lovers.

Ash

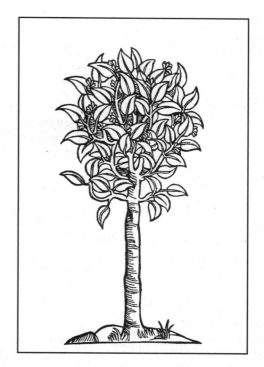

LIKE THE birch and the rowan, the ash tree thrives high up on exposed hills. The tree is easily recognized by its pure gray bark and large spreading crown especially after its leaves have fallen. The ash comes to leaf as late as May and loses its leaves by early October.

The Greeks dedicated the ash tree to Poseidon, god of the sea, and sailors carried its wood as protection against the threat of drowning. The major spiritual significance of the ash tree comes from Northern Europe, where as *Yggdrasil*, the World Tree, it connects the underworld, earth and heaven. The ash is associated in Norse myths with Odin (Woden), supreme among gods, who sought to increase his wisdom with extreme suffering. It was on an ash tree that he hanged himself:

> *Nine whole nights on a*
> *wind-rocked tree,*
> *Wounded with a spear,*
> *I was offered to Odin,*
> *myself to myself,*
> *On that tree that none*
> *may ever know*
> *What root beneath it runs.*

This account is recorded in the *Elder Edda*, Icelandic poems dating from about the tenth century.

Ash keys, so-called because they resemble keys used in medieval locks, are the winged seed pods dispersed by winter winds to form new trees. They are of value as fertility charms. Ash is one of the few woods that will burn easily and steadily when still green. Divination fires are often of green ash.

The Norns, mistresses of fate, tend the World Ash Tree – Yggdrasil.

Osoosi

Tracker in the Night

THE Yoruba of Southwestern Nigeria have long honored a pantheon of deities, the Orishas, that often embody many natural and esoteric phenomena. Encountering the Orisha Osoosi is to meet the spirit of the forest and its inhabitants. In this unique being we encounter an Orisha who not only embodies the spirit of the animals, but also that of the hunter who takes sustenance in the forest. Osoosi acts as the guardian for both, a paradox but not unique in the world of Orisha.

Osoosi is the divine hunter whose arrows never miss their mark. His ability to track game is unsurpassed by any and only equaled by Ogun, the other Orisha hunter in the pantheon. Yet Osoosi's ability is different from that of Ogun's. Osoosi is stealthy, cunning and magical; Ogun has extraordinary strength.

When we come across Osoosi, we find an Orisha whose beauty, refinement and intelligence comes shining through the rough nature of the skins that cover his body and bamboo shoots that serve as his hunting skirt. This association of skins has survived in Diaspora, in that like him, his objects in Diaspora are sometimes hidden beneath pelts of animals. Yet under the rough skins, lies a shrine whose objects can only be hewn in the in civility of a smithy.

The reality is that Osoosi is an Orisha straddling the world of civilization and the wild. He is an Orisha squarely in the court of Obatala, the Orisha of peace. Like Obatala, Osoosi favors white foods and oils. While his shrines are feral in nature – brambles surround his sacred objects, the bow and the arrow – Osoosi is treated to the same shea butter and white chalks as the other funfun (white) Orishas, avoiding the heat of palm oil and peppery foods. In fact, Osoosi's association with Obatala is so strong it is said that Obatala gave him the copper and brass with which to fashion his bows and arrows.

Osoosi, while knowing the fineness of civilization, chooses to be alone in his quest, remaining only half tamed. Yet he was not always so, as we see in this story:

Osoosi was the most skilled of hunters among the Orisha. Unlike his brother Ogun, Osoosi used intellect and speed instead of brute strength. One day he was out hunting when he happened upon a beautiful pair of birds, which he quickly snared and brought home.  Knowing that these birds would not be enough to feed his whole family, he strung up the birds and went back out on the hunt. While he further hunted, his mother came to his home and noticed the birds and decided that she would clean the birds and get them ready for the evening meal. When Osoosi returned, he immediately noticed that the two birds were missing. Infuriated that a thief would dare take his catch, he drew an arrow from his quiver and launched it into the air with bow, invoking, "May this arrow strike straight at the heart of whoever took my birds." As the arrow met its mark, he heard the wail from his mother as she gasped her last breath. Osoosi's heart was broken when he realized his deed. Indeed his sorrow was so deep that he retreated into the forest and only communed with the very animals that he hunted.

Because of Osoosi's remorse and retreat, he is associated with justice in the Diaspora. His self-imposed exile in many ways becomes a prison. It is in this way that Osoosi has become associated with jails and meting out of justice. In fact, prisons are referred to as "the house of Osoosi." In the Diaspora it is not uncommon to find among his sacred objects a set of handcuffs and guns. When problems with justice and law arise, devotees in the West will make offering to Osoosi, giving him his favored drink of anisette and preparing a dish of black-eyed peas.

Osoosi's loner trait also has a deeply esoteric side. Because he is a solitary figure in the wild, he is also said to have a shamanlike nature, associated with magical knowledge. His outward trait of being able to track game turns inward, allowing him to track Ase (spiritual essence). Inherent in his name is magic in and of itself. "Oso" the Yoruba word for wizard forms the first part of his name, "Osi" or left hand being the second part of his name. He is the Left handed Sorcerer. While the left hand is often associated with disturbing forces in the Yoruba pantheon, this is not the case with Osoosi. In this case it is indicative of his ability to see and use energies that are deeply magical. It also represents the ability of the Osoosi energy to access the unconscious side of being. His name is also related to the word for a night watchman – Osowusi. Both of these words point to his ability as a seer and knower of esoteric knowledge.

The metaphor of the forest dweller is of one who can track into a space that is other-worldly and does not live by the rules of the civilized world. It is in every way anathema to the urbane. Only those whose medicine is strong can survive in the forest. In the very prosaic world of a hunter, adorning yourself with pelts and feathers is necessary in order to be camouflaged. In the world of the sorcerer, the camouflage allows you to pass between the worlds and become one with the hunted – not to kill, but to work magic. His arrow cuts through detritus connecting to its mark in a straight and narrow path. His arrow is the metaphor converting will into intent. This is the object of the sorcerer the world over.

In the Diaspora, the sacred attributes of Osoosi include the bow and arrow, as is the case in West Africa. Added to these symbols are various hunting objects – spears, machetes, knives and the like, as well as the antlers and shins of deer. All of this clearly connects Osoosi with his hunter roots of West Africa. Also included in some Orisha lineages is an animal horn filled with medicine and capped with a mirror. This mirror is used by the Osoosi as means of divining. Again we have the connection of Osoosi to sorcery. Among the Yoruba, water or mirror gazing falls into the domain of the witches' and sorcerers' symbols.

Also inherent in the traits of Osoosi is the inability to confine the energy of the hunter/sorcerer. On a mundane level, this manifests in the fact that the natural-born hunter, while he may be adept in society, will always seek out the fenceless wild. This is the case even if the hunter does not plan to hunt; he communes with the beings that are known to him. He sits to observe and his curiosity drives him to know more. On an esoteric level, this represents the inability to tame the shaman. While the

shaman must exist within the world or mankind, he must be able to escape in order to serve mankind. The shaman is the seeker on the edges.

This living on the edge, again is reflected in the Diaspora. During the initiation period, most initiates are confined to a very small area within the sacred precinct. This area is dressed with fine fabrics and looks very much like a throne room in medieval Europe. The initiates are said to be crowned and are treated as royal. While Osoosi will also be treated in this manner, he will have another abode which is made outside under the sky. Like all the warrior Orisha, he will be "crowned" both inside and outside. He can not be kept within the confines of a "throne." He will be allowed to leave his inside throne and travel about as he pleases. His igba (sacred pot) will not sit on shelving, but will sit on a stump of his sacred tree, the almond – the same stump on which the initiate was crowned.

For those who wish to honor Osoosi at an unconsecrated altar, below are some of his attributes:
• Objects – Osoosi owns all things associated with hunting and fishing. This can include antlers, arrows, bows, and a small mirror.
• Colors – In many traditions Osoosi's colors are amber and blue. He can also be treated to green, brown and coral.
• Other attributes – Often hats and shoulder bags made of animal skins can be used to treat Osoosi.
• Offerings – Smoked fish, a mash of black-eyed peas.

The Yoruba of Southwestern Nigeria have long honored a pantheon of deities, the Orishas, that often embody many natural and esoteric phenomena. We encounter the Orisha Osoosi, the spirit of the forest and its inhabitants, in the current Witches' Almanac. One can sing the praise of Osoosi using his special Oriki (praise poem):

Ode onjia
Sese lehin aso
Ee ko po de
Oju li o ri egbin ko fo
Ojo po iya ma bi
A kere togbonsinon
Ode k oto ku agbanli
O si idi bata leri ebe
Ode nwo mi eru nba mi

Hunter who is a fighter
One who incessantly is a step behind the malcontent
You can not be bound
Your eyes look upon foulness and are unaffected
You do not bring suffering nor vomit
He is not vigorous, but is intelligent
Hunter who does not provoke death
He sits down in the field of other
Hunter you look at me and I feel fear

May your tracking bring sustenance and luck.

— IFADOYIN SANGOMUYIWA
Nigerian Priest to Sango and
Babalawo, Father of Secrets

Ifadoyin lives in New Jersey, where he also maintains
a spiritual house. He can be contacted directly,
through his website www.irunmole.org.

Merry Meetings

A candle in the window, a fire on the hearth,
a discourse over tea...

Forty years ago Paul Huson wrote the groundbreaking *Mastering Witchcraft,* and for most of the time the book has remained in print. Paul Huson is a true occult master producing a variety of classic works that have lasted the test of time. Last fall Paul agreed to speak with us about his early occult training and his love of tarot. It is our privilege to bring our readers Paul Huson's story in his own words.

What was your motivation to write Mastering Witchcraft *and how long did it take to put it all together?*

My interest in witchcraft in general and magic in particular started at about age ten, when I found that I could scry naturally and apparently cast spells when my intention was sufficiently solid. I guess you could say I started putting *Mastering Witchcraft* together when I began writing my own book of shadows in 1954, after reading Gerald Gardner's first book. My main research really took place between 1959 and 1963, when, as an undergraduate of London University,

Paul Huson at time of writing
Mastering Witchcraft

I had the library of the Folklore Society available to me. While I was studying art and design at the Slade School of Fine Art, I used to haunt the folklore library in my off hours – at that time it was housed in the main building of University College.

I emigrated from the U.K. to the States in 1968, hoping to find work in the film industry as an art director, as this had been my career in England. At the time there was supposed to be a reciprocal agreement between the U.S. and U.K. film and TV unions, but on arriving in Los Angeles I had found this not to be the case. It was one of those closed shop deals – you had to have done some design work in the States to get accepted into the union, but you couldn't actually get a job unless you were already in the union. In any case, art directing was not really my idea of a wonderful career, so at the time I never even gave a thought to the idea of using a spell to attract work. Friends suggested I write a book. "Witchcraft" seemed to be in the air at the time, so I wrote a couple of chapters and an outline based on my research. A friend gave it to an agent at William Morris, who thought it reasonable enough to pass on to the literary department in New York, and it was sold in short order to Putnams. The actual text and illustrations took me about three months to complete, I believe.

What contact, if any, did you have with practitioners of witchcraft or magic before writing Mastering Witchcraft?

After reading Gardner's books when they came out in 1954, I had written to him when I was fifteen, asking if he knew of a group where I could study magic formally, giving him details of magical experiments I had carried out. Interested, he wrote back, invited me to meet him "for a yarn," and mentioned the Society of the Inner Light as the best place to get a training in magic, although he doubted they'd take anyone my age. Any more occult adventuring on my part, however, was abruptly curtailed at this point by the discovery of school séances I had been organizing. The headmaster took a dim view of them, believing them to be diabolical in inspiration, which they were not, and threatened me, as the instigator, with immediate expulsion should he so much as even catch me reading an occult book in the future. So my wings were clipped for the time being.

However as soon as I left boarding school to attend the Slade in 1959, I applied to the SIL, Society of the Inner Light, for membership. Contrary to Gardner's expectations, I was accepted as a candidate for their mail order training course. At this time it involved

Paul Huson while studying with the Society of Inner Light

reading the society material, and once a fortnight answering questions on it, performing daily meditations on various set subjects and submitting your meditation log and replies to the question sheet to a mentor at the society for inspection. All this was designed to not only teach the student, but to draw him or her into the group's egregore and aid him or her in picking up the contacts the SIL worked at that time. I discovered that someone named Arthur Chichester was to be my mentor, although I had no idea at the time that he was the Society's warden. I completed the first part of the course, apparently to his satisfaction.

However I began finding the material inconsistent and in some places self-contradictory, notably the Qabalistic material, which I had been fairly well versed in before I applied for membership, which clashed with the more theosophical type of "cosmic doctrine" material propagated by the Society. I voiced my problems to Chichester and he made light of them, suggesting I was just reacting to the "form" of the teaching, but that basically everything

Witchgods – *Illustration by Paul Huson for* Mastering Witchcraft

was consistent. However I could not rid myself of my skepticism, this has been a recurring issue all my life, I find and rightly surmised that I couldn't continue working with the group while in that frame of mind. So that was the end of the SIL for me; materially, at least. However I'm fairly sure I'd picked up some of their contacts.

Could you elaborate on what sort of contacts you reference? Are these spirit guides, godforms?

Godforms. The SIL taught that the form of the shaggy-hooved Great God Pan was a powerful symbol of "the divine as manifested through nature." As a painter and designer, I was drawn to what the society called the Orphic or "Green Ray" path, which used the symbolism of European myth and folklore – Etruscan, Celtic, Nordic, which for me meant Aradia, Cernunnos, Odin, Freya, Weyland, and later forms like the fairy

folk and Holda, Habondia, and Hertha – to make inner-plane contacts.

Were there specific sources that you can identify as being the main influences on the tone and style of the book?

Barham's *Ingoldsby Legends* and Jack Vance's writings, I should think. I felt that a book about witchcraft should not only be informative, but stimulate the imagination of the reader, cast its own spell, so to speak. Books on occult subjects until then always seemed to me to tend toward the turgid, which is something I was anxious to avoid.

How much of your work for Mastering Witchcraft *was pure research, and how much was revealed as a result of meditation or praxis?*

The "witch power" produced from what I called the Witches' Pyramid, i.e., the force that aids the operator to achieve the necessary inner plane or Deep Mind contact to work magic, was a working concept I evolved from following clues given by Albertus Magnus, Agrippa, Paracelsus, Levi, Crowley, and yes, even Gardner himself. It forms the basis for the success of any of the rituals. As to the rituals' origins, I would answer half research, half the result of my own "ingenium," as Crowley would say. For instance, the elemental invocations were developed as a result of my own intuition and praxis, and the tool consecrations were pretty much Key of Solomon and Golden Dawn. So to answer your question, I would have to say *Mastering Witchcraft* was half pure research and half a result of meditation and praxis.

In Mastering Witchcraft *you mention watcher lore, Tubal Cain as the Witch God, Nahmaah and Lillith which are more commonly associated with traditional craft than with Gardner's Wica and the more eclectic forms of witchcraft prevalent today. Did your encounters with associates of Robert Cochrane, who is best known as a proponent of traditional witchcraft, expose you to these concepts or had you encountered them via other venues?*

The lore to which you refer I acquired as a result of my own personal research and meditation. During my meetings with folk like Bill Gray, I was only presented with interesting minutiae, like the correct method to visualize the Interior Castle or how to use the image of the blue periwinkle as the flower of death – none of the basic materials or godforms. I was surprised, not to say intrigued, when a certain Joe Wilson wrote to me after he had read *Mastering Witchcraft* and informed me how much it apparently contained of Cochrane's teachings. I can only assume that I had picked up the Cochrane folk's egregore/group mind while I was in their company.

There have been rumors of association with Alex Sanders and other Wiccans. I know you have previously answered this particular question in an online forum, but that posting is long gone and I believe this venue provides an opportunity to get your answer out to a wider audience. The question of your "origins" comes up over and over. I'd like to have your position on the issue to stand as a definitive answer.

I was not the "Paul" mentioned in June Johns's account of Sanders's life, nor did I ever have the pleasure of meeting Sanders, or to my knowledge any of his folk, although maybe they were present at some of Tamara's salons. For the record, I have never been initiated into any coven, and I have certainly never broken any secrecy oaths.

In the years since the publication of Mastering Witchcraft, *witchcraft has undergone a modern renaissance and there are now hundreds of books on the subject and many differing groups practicing a variety of forms both traditional and modern. Do you have any regular contact with practicing witches or traditions?*

I keep in fairly regular contact with Nigel Jackson, and used to have sporadic contact with Joe Wilson until he died.

How do you see your role in promoting the resurgence of interest in witchcraft over the last forty years?

Preliminary drawings by Paul Huson for The Fool and Justice, Dame Fortune's Wheel Tarot

85

I guess I was the first writer to present the general public with a practical guide to witchcraft rituals at a time when it was almost impossible to gain that kind of information unless you were initiated into a coven or lodge. I gather *Mastering Witchcraft* remained an influential book over the years, despite opposition from fundamentalist Christians and Gardnerian Wiccans of the "Wiccan Rede" persuasion. I didn't pull any punches in the book, and folk like Farrar took pains to label it amoral, if not immoral. Wiccan Reders also latched onto my use of the word "warlock" as somehow significant; warlock of course is a perfectly standard Scottish term for a male witch and has nothing to do with oath-breaking or coven excommunication or any of that kind of folderol you find bandied about on the Net.

Have you considered writing a sequel or an updated version of Mastering Witchcraft?

No. As for a sequel, I think the field is somewhat oversaturated, and my interests have moved on since then.

You have also authored two books on the subject of the tarot, The Devil's Picture Book *and* Mystical Origins of the Tarot. *I also understand that a tarot deck* Dame Fortune's Wheel Tarot *is in production. In your view how does the tarot fit into the world view and practice of the witch?*

Although probably initially devised as a card game, from the sixteenth century, at least, I believe the tarot has been used in Europe as an instrument of divination. As such, it's a perfectly viable magical tool for those who work within what Dion Fortune used to call "the Western esoteric tradition." The trumps and court cards reflect a medieval Catholic Christian world view, but it is a Christianity that has clothed its simple gospel tale in a garment of classical paganism and Neo-Platonism, and as such presents images resonant to Christian and pagan alike.

Haunting good libraries is a fine way to satisfy the yearning for learning no matter what the subject matter may be. For such adventurous seekers or even the more experienced readers among the stacks, what advice would you give about structuring a self-directed curriculum to help aid the greater journey on the esoteric path?

People have their own inner needs which only they can identify. Obviously these needs are what should direct their book research. Without knowing the person, it's impossible to give advice to someone, especially on esoteric matters. There are so many different paths, so much literature available today.

– OWEN ROWLEY

For additional interview questions, visit our website, www.TheWitchesAlmanac. com/AlmanacExtras.

Paul Huson, 2004

The Fleur-de-Lis

Flower of Power

THE FLEUR-DE-LIS has proclaimed royalty on shields, scepters, crowns and coins, expressing the belief that kings ruled by divine right. The emblem has descended through cultures and spanned ages. Today it is indiscriminately used as an ornament while still representing France, the Boy Scouts, New Orleans and Florence, Italy. Its shape has been interpreted as an iris, a lily, a toad, a ladybug, Baphomet, and the trinity of faith, wisdom and chivalry. Early examples of the fleur-de-lis existed in ancient Egypt, Greece, Sumer, Crete and Rome, each unfailingly resurrecting the mystery of life, transformation, death and rebirth.

Most recently this icon gained attention in the controversial novel *The Da Vinci Code* as the brand of the secret society Priory of Scion, guardians of the living Holy Grail. Although the book is fictional, the legend is based on a popular and often debunked theory espoused in *Holy Blood, Holy Grail.* It was believed that the Grail, with a purpose to serve mankind, was a living vessel embodied in Mary Magdalene. Mary Magdalene reportedly arrived in France impregnated with Jesus's descendant and progenitor of the line of Merovingian kings.

The emblem of Clovis I

The Merovingians ruled Western continental Europe, including France, throughout the early Middle Ages, and several chronicles exist to account for why the fleur-de-lis represents that bloodline. Clovis I, the Merovingian founder of the Frankish kingdom, reportedly agreed to convert to Christianity if he won the battle of Tolbiac in 496 C.E. Although Clovis did win the battle and convert, the legends of his heraldic adoption didn't originate until the fourteenth century. These tales report that the emblem was bestowed upon Clovis I by either a hermit, an anointing angel, through a magical transformation of his shield's pagan toads, or as a bargain made with his Christian wife and the Roman Catholic Church.

Clovis I was the first king to obtain the Christian church's recognition of a king's divine right to rule. It was a brilliant strategy, subjugating the church and the people to Clovis' rule in an age when Christianity was growing politically powerful. Nevertheless the first record associating Clovis' fleur-de-lis heraldry with Christianity was over six hundred years after his adoption of the new religion.

Madonna lily

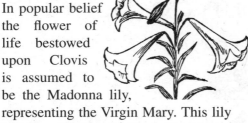

In popular belief the flower of life bestowed upon Clovis is assumed to be the Madonna lily, representing the Virgin Mary. This lily is said to have sprung from Eve's tears as she left the Garden of Eden. The Madonna lily's first recorded association with Jesus's mother was in 1223 C.E., symbolizing purity and the trinity. In Latin *lis* is plural for *lil*, denoting purity or whiteness. The cross-association of the lily and emblem with the Virgin Mary and Mary Magdalene may be remnants of a mother-wife goddess who had several relationships to her consort, such as Osiris and Isis.

A second-century Gaulish coin displays a woman holding a lily. The flower's leaves signify a lily as opposed to an iris, and its design elements bear strong similarities to the fleur-de-lis. But as being Clovis' yellow fleur-de-lis, the association is questionable due to the Madonna lily's white color and because yellow lilies were historically uncommon.

Resurrection motifs

Clovis' original pagan shield design is said to have depicted toads. Some see the toad's transformation as a metamorphosis into the fleur-de-lis, the toad's body becoming the flower's stamen and its legs the petals. This theory is not as farfetched as it may seem. Many cultures use toads as symbols of regeneration and truth, a recurring pattern in the fleur's associations. The toad's wondrous life cycle reflects the alchemist's search for everlasting life, shape shifting from egg to tadpole to pollywog to adult – all forms of the same being transubstantiated. The toad also buries itself in winter and resurrects in the spring.

Middle Ages Europe associated toads with evil, poison, witchcraft and familiars, but that wasn't always the case. Ancient Egyptians entombed mummified toads with pharaohs, whom they considered gods personified. Egyptian hieroglyphics often represent toads with the tree of life springing from their backs. Could Clovis' toads have similarly fertilized the fleur-de-lis?

The tree of everlasting life plays a major role in the powerful resurrection myth of Osiris. Set tricks Osiris into a chest and dumps him in the Nile. Eventually Osiris' coffin drifts ashore at the foot of a tamarisk tree in Phoenicia, where in time he becomes encased in its trunk and carved into a palace's pillar. The pillar's sweet scent gains such regard that Isis hears of the phenomenon and recognizes the presence of Osiris. Isis restores him to her side and though already dead, bears Osiris a child in virgin birth.

Osiris' crown closely resembles the fleur-de-lis. Some say it symbolizes three feathers of truth, the center being the *axis mundi* or world tree. As the "Pillar of Heaven," Osiris' roots reach to the netherworld and branch to the stars.

Variations of Osiris' myth existed in Sumer and many other cultures. The tree worshiping Franks certainly could have related to this horticultural regeneration story, having clearly believed in reincarnation. Is it coincidence that British excavations have uncovered toads embedded within the bowls of tree trunks?

Irises, bees, toads

Another theory is that Clovis' pagan heraldry was based on designs of bees, flies or ladybugs. Clovis' father, King Childeric, died in 481 C.E. and his tomb was discovered in 1653. Three hundred golden-insect icons were immured in it and his remains were draped in a cloth decorated with the creatures. Some bifoliated versions of Osiris' crown resemble a fleur-de-lis similar to Childeric's insects. Osiris' crown is also reflected in the shape of a court jester's hat, the British two-pence piece and the three feathered Prince of Wales' crown with the underlying motto "I serve," which parallels the purpose of the Grail.

King Clovis' actual adopted heraldry resembles a golden flower similar to the European iris. Like Osiris' coffin and the toad, it is amphibious, growing in the rivers and marshes spanned by the Merovingian Empire, most notably the river Lis.

The iris plant was actually called a lily until the nineteenth century. The seventeenth-century herbalist Nicholas Culpeper calls it the "Flower de Luce." The native European yellow iris, *Iris pseudacorus*, is under the moon's dominion. Other common names include yellow flag, water flag, sword flag or in German, *lieschblume.* In France the iris is popularly called *flambé* or *flame* – the French battle standard was called the *oriflamme.*

In Greek, "iris" means rainbow and *eiris*, herald. Iris is the beautiful golden-winged goddess of the rainbow who is draped in saffron and carries a pitcher and a herald's caduceus. She travels at the speed of the wind, plummeting to the underworld river Styx to fill her ewer with water for dousing perjurers. Iris supplies the clouds with water and her colorful bow spans the sky, uniting earth to heaven. She is the messenger of the gods to man and serves as envoy for Zeus and Hera. The fleur-de-lis is also Hera's personal flower, springing from the tip of her staff like a scepter.

The yellow iris returns us to Childric's golden insects as bumblebees, honeybees and hover flies, pollinators of the wild iris. Other names for the insects include *lucifera* ("light bringers"), *lisses, luces,* "*lucies* bees," scarabs, "*scara* bees" or imperial bees of Charlemagne (a Merovingian). The plant's roots, an antidote to poison, are used in Roman purification ceremonies, and Pliny cautions that these should only be harvested by the chaste.

Flower of destiny

Universally the myth of the hero predestined for great acts is an archetypal character typically of virgin birth, such as Jesus, Horus or Athena. The divine right of kings asserts that such a singular birthright bestows the bloodline with royal larger-than- life status.

A far older legend of the Merovingian blooline exists. Meroveus, the progenitor, was said to be sired by the Quinotaur, Neptune's half-bull, half-fish sea-god or demigod. This gives credence to some claims that the fleur-de-lis is Neptune's stylized trident and another explanation of why the emblem would top

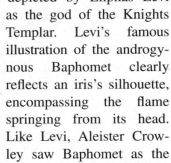

a scepter. The myth of the bloodline of the Merovingian kings exemplifies an archetypal virgin birth motif that seems to have transcended from one age's popular religion to the next. In it, a child is born of divinity and predestined to become the champion of the people.

The fleur-de-lis also adorns the crowns of England and Scotland. Some crown designs even mimic an iris flower's shape. Ruskin called it the flower of chivalry, having "a sword for its leaf and a lily for its heart."

A less clear relationship exists between the fleur-de-lis and Baphomet of Mendes, the goat-headed god with the flame of illumination between his horns depicted by Eliphas Levi as the god of the Knights Templar. Levi's famous illustration of the androgynous Baphomet clearly reflects an iris's silhouette, encompassing the flame springing from its head. Like Levi, Aleister Crowley saw Baphomet as the divine androgyne. The Rosicrucians are also reported to associate the fleur-de-lis with self-begetting, self-producing generative power.

Considering all such complex associations with the fleur-de-lis, it may never be possible to draw a firm conclusion about which exact flower the emblem represents or whether it was intended to depict a flower at all. The conclusions that can be drawn are mythic and archetypal. The power of the fleur-de-lis leads us consistently down the trail to the hero's virgin birth, transformation, death and rebirth.

– NIALLA NI MACHA

Thou art the Iris, fair among the fairest,
Who, armed with golden rod
And winged with the celestial azure, bearest
The message of some God.
Thou art the Muse, who far from crowded cities
Hauntest the sylvan streams,
Playing on pipes of reed the artless ditties
That come to us as dreams.

O flower de luce, bloom on, and let the river
Linger to kiss thy feet!
O flower of song, bloom on, and make forever
The world more fair and sweet.

– *Henry Wadsworth Longfellow*, Flower de Luce

Wedding Ceremonies

A feast of marriage customs

TODO MARRIAGE seems a natural outcome for two individuals in love. Not long ago, marriages were arranged by the heads of families – and in some cultures they still are. The young bride was regarded as property and her marriage was a bill of sale. The modern father walking his daughter down the isle mimics what was once a fact. The transaction was completed by the father tapping the bride on her head with her shoe and then handing it to the groom.

As recently as one hundred fifty years ago in England a husband could sell a wife he was unhappy with. In 1832 after three years of marriage Joseph Thomson put a straw halter on his wife and sold her for twenty shillings and a dog.

Not all weddings were arranged. Some brides were abducted. The honeymoon is derived from the first "honey month" a couple spent hiding. With any luck, the new husband would have impregnated his wife by the time her family found them.

In Elizabethan England, the church's practice of announcing upcoming weddings at three different times served as a community notice to any prior bedmates that might be pregnant with the evidence to object. This may have occurred with William Shakespeare, whose marriage banns announced his upcoming marriage to Anne Whateley but later married the pregnant Anne Hathaway. This may have been a clerical mistake or it could shed light on Shakespeare bequeathing his "second best bed" to his wife.

The wedding date was an important decision. Farm families know that a waxing-to-full-moon is prime. Maritime families lived by the fortunes of the sea and knew that getting married during high tide was a bad omen. Other families that didn't live by the moon surely lived by the clock, preferring the portion of the hour when the minute hand is rising.

In the same spirit of contradiction, some weather lore alleges that rain on the wedding day yields many tears, while the Norse considered a storm a good fertility omen. Contradictory customs also effect the wedding date. In Rome, May was dedicated to Maia, the goddess of old age and death; June was dedicated to Juno, the goddess of marriage.

Tradition offers many charms and amulets for the nuptial couple. Mother

Goose contains a popular wedding charm for a happily married life:

Something old, something new
Something borrowed, something blue
And a silver sixpence in your shoe.

Each verse is an ingredient to a bride's happiness – her old friends and family, her new husband, the borrowed luck of a happily married women, a blue item for fidelity and a silver sixpence to ensure the couple's prosperity. The sixpence is swapped for a penny in the United States. Considering that copper is ruled by Venus, the bringer of love and wealth, this adaptation should work quite well.

If the prior charm doesn't suit, there is always the nefarious version:

Something new, something old,
Something borrowed, something
  stoled.

In some countries couples remove their old clothes and don new ones to symbolize their transition into a new life. A curious deviation of this custom was once practiced in England. If a bride arrived at a groom's door naked, or depending on local tradition, in an undergarment, the groom could marry her without taking on her debts. During the nineteenth century, a bride in Kirton-on-Lindsey in Lancashire, England reportedly descended a ladder from her bedroom window stark naked before changing her mind.

The modern preference for a white gown began with Queen Victoria in 1840:

Married in White,
  you have chosen right,
Married in Blue,
  your love will always be true,
Married in Pearl,
  you will live in a whirl,
Married in Brown,
  you will live in town,
Married in Red,
  you will wish yourself dead,
Married in Yellow,
  ashamed of your fellow,
Married in Green,
  ashamed to be seen,
Married in Pink,
  your spirit will sink,
Married in Grey,
  you will go far away,
Married in Black,
  you will wish yourself back.

One of the earliest records of placing the wedding ring on what has become the customary finger was in Lucrezia Borgia's 1493 betrothal contract to Giovanni Sforza. The document provided that the ring was to be put on her left finger "whose vein leads to the heart." Unfortunately for him, that

belief wasn't true. Early Jewish rings were inscribed with the Hebrew *mazal tov*, "good fortune."  Puritans disapproved of wedding rings for their "heathenish origin" as a "Relique of Popery and a Diabolical Circle for the Devil to Dance with." The use of diamonds was considered evil as well because they interrupted the ring's circle, indicating that a spouse's regard might not be perpetually reciprocated.

Knots were a form of binding magic commonly used in courtships. A couple in ancient Rome "tied the knot" by binding their images together while reciting their vows. Knot magic was considered so powerful that in the Middle Ages wedding couples untied any knots in their clothing before the ceremony. Another form of knot magic was used to confuse the Evil Eye into unravelling each knot in the wedding veil, preventing it from focusing on the bride. Young Irishmen plaited straw into true-lovers knots, which they gave to their intended. If their love was reciprocated, their intended would pin it to her bosom.

Scottish couples made stoles or capes from a fur the man had trapped and cured himself. The couple stitched it to a silk lining and stowed a lock of pubic hair in each end – the man's on the right and the woman's on the left. It was worn so that each end crossed over her heart.

Bundling was once common, giving the couple a test run of married life by allowing the young man to spend nights in his betrothed's bed with a bundling board separating them. Though expected to respect the custom of chastity, sometimes pregnancies and ensuing marriages resulted. Bundling was practiced by the Puritans in New England into the eighteenth century. A similar version is still practiced in Holland, where the young woman is armed with tongs and an iron vessel to protect herself from unwanted attention should the young man breaking through her window be unwelcome or too forward.

A handfasted couple's trial wedding is considered "more than engaged and less than married." If no child results

from living together for a year and a day, they could separate. Otherwise they married. This practice once spanned from Ireland to Norway, and is still observed in Staphurst, Holland. The custom of tying hands together at handfastings and weddings has enjoyed a resurgence among neopagans. Czech couples employ this technique by joining hands above their head. Each women in the wedding party takes a ribbon and dances in one direction and the men in the other. When the couple's forearms are tied, they are married.

Magically sweeping an area of evil spirits and negative influences away has been practiced from Africa to ancient Peru. The powers of the broom protect African couples as they jump it into married life. The ritual is concluded with the officiant reading something like this traditional slave marriage poem:

Dark and stormy may
come the weather,
This man and woman
are joined together.
Let none but him that
makes the thunder,
Put this man and woman asunder.
I therefore announce you
both the same,
Be good, go long, and
keep up your name.
The broomstick's jumped, the
world's not wide,
She's now yours, go kiss your bride!

A similar symbolism is expressed in Jewish marriages. The couple drink wine from the same glass in recognition of the good times ahead, then smash it as a reminder of coming hardships and the fragility of their bond.

In a beautiful Indian wedding tradition the couple offers each other the loving cup and as they gaze into a mirror they are asked, "What do you see?" Each responds, "I see the rest of my life."

Wedding feasts around the world treat the newlyweds to foods symbolic of their future together. An adapted Yoruba ceremony combines lemon, vinegar, cayenne and honey to represent the sour, bitter, spicy and sweet flavors of married life.

The Polish practice of passing the wedding cake through a wedding ring nine times to divine the couple's future became so popular the church banned it in 1279 C.E. Another divination is made by placing a piece of cake or "dreaming-bread" under an unmarried woman's pillow to dream of her future mate. In some parts of Britain the groom still breaks a plate over the bride's head as they leave the church. Breaking the plate into many pieces foretells many children. Throwing grain like rice or dried fruits on the newlyweds also is intended to bless them with fertility.

The Scots prevail in preventing difficulties during the early days of wedlock. By customarily marrying on December 31, the couple can arise the next morning and honestly claim they have been married for over a year and never had a quarrel. The whole world celebrates their anniversary with them, and chances are that they will never forget the date!

– LILLIAN GENTRY

Friday the 13th

Are you paraskavedekatriaphobic or what?

EACH YEAR has at least one. Some years have as many as three of these mystical and controversial days. "Paraskavedekatriaphobic" is the impressive title for one who fears Friday the 13th. If the syllables bowl you over, think of the term this way: *paraskave* is the Greek word for Friday; *dekatria* is Greek for 13 (*deka*, 10; *tria*, 3). Statistics reveal that up to 21 million Americans may have a dread so severe that it affects work and business transactions to the tune of millions of dollars in lost wages and revenue every time the day rolls around. In Britain a survey shows significantly more traffic accidents on these Fridays.

Most of us have some feelings, for good or ill, about the number thirteen and about Friday the 13th in particular. Accepting a new job, walking under a ladder, watching a black cat cross our path can be omens of either delight or terror. An overall terror of the number 13 is "paraskavedekatriaphobia"; people who delight in the number are "paraskavedekatriaphiles." In the Middle Ages humble bakers, afraid of being accused of short-changing a powerful customer on a dozen rolls, would wisely add one extra for goodwill and personal safety. A "baker's dozen" has been synonymous with a lucky and protective thirteenth item ever since.

The intriguing chain of lore connected to Friday the 13th includes misfortune for the Knights Templar – members of the Order faced arrest on Friday, October 13, 1307. (The incident speeds the plot in the historical novel, *The DaVinci Code*.) In 1869 the first reference to this date being bad luck occurs in print. The biography of Gioahino Rossini reveals that he feared Friday the 13th and died on that date in November, 1869.

During the twentieth century superstitions and beliefs about the number 13, especially Friday the 13th in particular, were widely embraced. An 1898 *Dictionary of Phrase and Fable* labels both Friday and Thirteen unlucky in separate entries. All English-speaking nations, Latin America, Scandinavia, Germany, Austria, Belgium, Poland and the Philippines have traditions and customs recognizing this date, each in its own national manner.

Dire events, Friday the 13th

- Friday, January 13, 1939 – Australia's Black Friday. Brush fires caused widespread damage.
- Friday, October 13, 1972 – The plane carrying Uruguay's entire winning Olympic rugby team crashed into the Andes mountains. That same day the musical group Black Sabbath debuted a landmark album.
- Friday, October 13, 2006 – Lemony Snicket's 13th book in "A Series of Unfortunate Events" was released. That same day a severe Friday the 13th storm struck Buffalo, New York.
- Friday, June 13, 2008 – Esteemed journalist Tim Russert died suddenly. He was 58 years old and 5 + 8 = 13.
- The release date on the latest in the series of Friday the 13th horror flicks draws on the date of February 13, 2009.
- Friday, April 13, 2029 – Looking further ahead. On this date Asteroid 99942, Apophis, will pass very close to Earth. If it makes landfall, its impact could create major climate and other changes affecting the entire planet.

Fearsome, felicitous – beliefs differ widely

In the tarot cards, 13 is Death in the Major Arcana. An omen of new beginnings and a glance into the world of the after-life, it is considered a good card. In pagan rites 13 witches are a full coven, while Christians link the 13 apostles at the Last Supper with death and betrayal. The Last Supper is thought to have taken place on a Friday, perhaps the root of the unlucky Friday the 13th concerns.

Mariners have their own stories. A Captain Friday set sail on a Friday the 13th on a ship named the "S.S. Friday." Neither captain, crew nor vessel was ever seen again. In Britain ships will not leave port on a Friday.

Meanings vary with the various religions. Thirteen Buddhas exist in the Indian pantheon; pagodas in the Far East are surmounted by 13 discs. A sacred sword at Japan's Atsusa Temple has 13 objects in its hilt. In Mexico 13 relates to the sacred snake gods. Film buffs might note that the 2008 *Indiana Jones and The Kingdom of the Crystal Skull* featured a circle of 13 crystal skulls with profound powers.

Many hotels don't have a 13th floor or room number and in Italian opera houses seats are never numbered 13.

The United States of America, the wealthiest and most privileged society that has ever existed, has 13 stripes on the flag, 13 stars and stripes on the

National Seal. The details of the Seal reveal more symbolism. The Eagle has 13 tail feathers in each wing and holds 13 arrows and 13 olive branches. Our national motto has 13 letters; 13 was the number of original colonies. Scholars attribute the number 13 to the mysteries of the Masonic practices which were the occult and spiritual beliefs held by the nation's founders. George Washington called for a 13-gun salute when he raised the flag for the first time.

Meditation for Friday the 13th

Mystics and adepts quietly smile and say, "Those who understand the number thirteen hold the keys of Power and Dominion." To unlock these legendary keys, light a black or silver candle. Add patchouli incense for a deeper focus. Place a skull motif and Tarot Key 13 motif upon the altar. Reflect on this meditation:

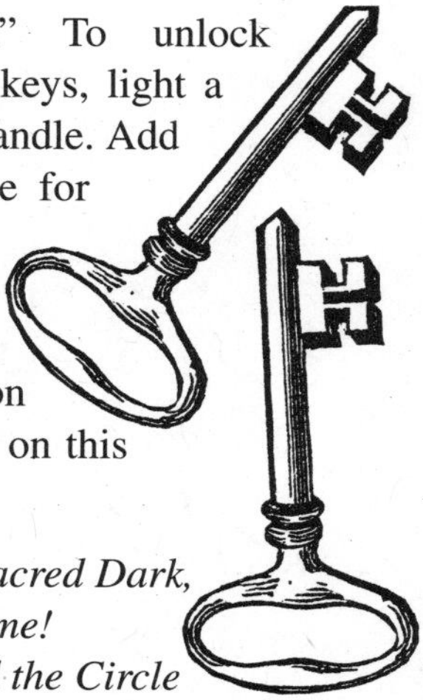

Radiant Light, Sacred Dark,
Lost in Magic Time!
Bring Us Around the Circle
Off beat Harmony, Vision. Welcome!
Break from the orderly, usual and expected!

— MARINA BRYONY

Friday the 13th Calendar
2010 – 2012

2010
August 13, 2010

2011
May 13, 2011

2012
January 13, 2012
April 13, 2012
July 13, 2012

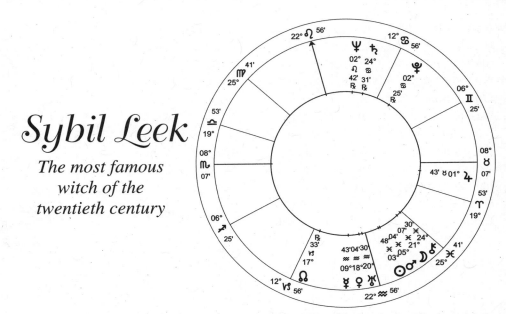

Sybil Leek

*The most famous
witch of the
twentieth century*

"I AM A WITCH." This simple, powerful statement is the opening line of the 1968 best-selling book, *Diary of a Witch*, by Sybil Leek. It gripped the hearts and minds of an entire generation of those drawn to follow the old ways of witchcraft.

The legendary Sybil Leek was among the first to popularize witchcraft, as well as astrology, herbal healing, crystals, tarot, numerology, mediumship, psychic phenomena and related subjects. Her work included dozens of books as well as television interviews, newspaper features and the magazine, "Sybil Leek's Astrology." Her achievements profoundly influenced the early years of the New Age and metaphysical movement. Today's witches enjoy a wider acceptance of their beliefs than craft practitioners at any time in history. For this we owe a debt of gratitude to Sybil, as she urged friends to call her.

Sybil was born on February 22, 1917, the birth date on cards given to mourners at her memorial service on October 29, 1982. (Several conflicting birth dates have been published, spanning 1916 to 1922). In her "Diary" Sybil describes her birthplace as a wild, desolate witch-ridden part of Staffordshire, England, at a crossroads where three rivers meet along the backbone of the Pennine Mountain range, the backbone of England. During mid-November of 1976, I was working for Sybil when she mentioned that the planet Uranus was transiting her ascendant that week. A glance at the ephemeris showed Uranus at 8 degrees of Scorpio, providing an accurate birth time of 11:40 p.m., just before the traditional witching hour of midnight. This zodiacal degree is linked to a high degree of intelligence, impatience, a passionate nature and strong emotions.

Sybil was born just after the New Moon, with both her Sun and Moon in the 4th house in Pisces. A New Moon in the horoscope of a famous individual often indicates one who becomes a symbol, an icon for an important movement. (For example, Queen Victoria, who became a representative for an entire historical cycle, and Clara Barton, whose life symbolizes the Red Cross, were also New Moon personalities.)

Sybil was proud of her family tree and described a lineage of witchcraft going back to the year 1134. She shared details of Russian and Irish occultists on both sides of her family, as well as a relationship with the seventeenth-century English witch Molly Leigh, who also practiced herbalism and magic in Staffordshire. Sybil also owned several antique shops and wrote delightful books about the antique business. This, along with Sybil's active involvement in real estate investments, can be seen in her strong natal 4th house, with Mars and Chiron forming a stellium including the Sun and Moon. She was close to both of her parents, proudly describing a psychic link with her father. Her mother, fondly known as Madame or Dame Louisa Fawcett, visited Sybil in Florida during the winter months. Louisa was familiar to Sybil's friends and neighbors. During the 1970s along Florida's Space Coast, they hobnobbed with local celebrities; their names were always popping up in the newspapers.

Sybil's applying Sun Mars conjunction trines her ascendant and describes her enthusiasm and energy as well as her infamous temper. Few people ever bested her in any kind of confrontation. The Pisces placements form a grand trine in water signs with Pluto and Saturn in Cancer and the Scorpio ascendant. While growing up Sybil described beach vacations in the South of France, where her family migrated to

escape the chilly English winters. She lived from the late 1960s until her death in Brevard County, Florida, in a variety of beach homes near the ocean or overlooking the Indian River. The powerful water sign influence describes her affinity for the waterfront. She was often seen strolling along the beach near sunset wearing flowing dresses billowing in the breeze, garments she designed and sewed herself. The strong accent on water signs also reveals Sybil's great sensitivity and her natural talent for attunement with the spirit realm.

Neptune, the dispositor or ruler of the Pisces planets, is in Leo in the 9th house. It is the chart's important hyleg, the elevated planet closest to the mid heaven. It is most significant that Neptune is in mutual reception with her Sun, making Sybil as much a Leo as a Pisces. Mutual receptions are especially fortunate influences in a natal chart. Having one reads the planets involved back in the other sign, adding extra depth and potential to the nativity. Mutual receptions offer an ability to change places, to get in and out of situations with aplomb. The flamboyant Leo energy was evident in her effervescent appearance. Sybil had a natural

star quality, usually wearing bright caftans accented with unusual jewelry. She created a memorable and dramatic presence wherever she went. Sybil's name was associated with figures in the entertainment world and such well-known authors as Hans Holzer and Jess Stern. She once said that she had been in the public eye since the age of sixteen.

Neptune makes an out of sign conjunction with Saturn, showing her hard work and dedication to the 9th house matters of travel, writing and spiritual studies. Sybil traveled around the world following a successful media career in England. She was largely self-educated and had only three years of formal schooling. Quite a storyteller, Sybil was often suspected of embellishing the details of her life as well as other matters. The Mercury Neptune opposition hints at this credibility issue. Her North Node in Capricorn in the 3rd house showed her ability to write and converse with ease, solving practical problems through information exchange.

Sybil's creativity, her appreciation for jewelry, art and music as well as her flair for communication are revealed by a conjunction of Mercury, Venus and Uranus in Aquarius in her 3rd house.

Her Jupiter in Taurus in the 6th house shows her interest in nature, including plants as well as her menagerie of pets. Sybil wrote of her childhood pet owl. Her fans grew to know of Mr. Hotfoot Jackson, her tame jackdaw (raven), Mr. Verdi Verdi, her iguana, as well as various beloved horses and cats. A tribe of beautiful Siamese cats wooed visitors, living happily in an enclosed patio at one of her Indialantic, Florida residences.

Venus ruled Taurus is on Sybil's 7th house of marriage. While she wrote romantically of her husbands, with Venus conjunct Uranus, her marriages didn't last. Leek scholars and close friends disagree as to whether she was married two or three times. She especially loved and admired those born under the sign of Virgo, the natural partner and opposing sign of Pisces. Both of her beloved sons, Stephen and Julian, are Virgos.

Sybil had fragile health and was frequently ill throughout her life. The 6th house Jupiter forms a fixed sign grand cross with Neptune, Mercury and the ascendant. She struggled with obesity and asthma before finally succumbing to cancer. There are several retrograde

planets, including Pluto, ruler of her ascendant. Pluto is in the 8th house. This hints at past life karma carried by the presence of a very old soul. Since her passing, spirit messages sent from Sybil have been received by a number of mediums.

Many of her planets are in cadent houses, which shows a progressive and futuristic outlook. Sybil lived a very intriguing life and was ahead of her time. Her legacy sets an example and provides inspiration. She paved the way for witches of present and future generations. Sybil Leek passed away on October 26, 1982, near Halloween, the most sacred time in the witches' year.

– DIKKI-JO MULLEN

Sybil Leek

Sybil Leek was born on February 22, 1917 at 11:40 p.m. UT in Staffordshire, UK 52 N 50, 002 W 00.

Data Table
(Tropical Placidus Houses)

Sun 3 Pisces 48 – 4th house

Moon 21 Pisces 07 – 4th house (New Moon)

Mercury 9 Aquarius 43 – 3rd house

Venus 18 Aquarius 04 – 3rd house

Mars 5 Pisces 04 – 4th house

Jupiter 1 Taurus 43 – 6th house

Saturn 24 Cancer 31 – 9th house (retrograde)

Uranus 20 Aquarius 30 – 3rd house

Neptune 2 Leo 42 – 9th house (retrograde)

Pluto 2 Cancer 25 – 8th house (retrograde)

Chiron 24 Pisces 30 – 4th house

N. Moon Node 17 Capricorn 33

Ascendant or Rising Sign is 8 degrees Scorpio 07

Cecil Williamson

Witchcraft Museum a lasting tribute

CECIL WILLIAMSON deserves to be better known to the occult community, an instrumental figure in the formation of the modern Wiccan/witchcraft movements. He was the founder of the Witchcraft Research Centre and a superb collector of artifacts that took him through fifty years of controversy. Today he is still remembered well in Boscastle, Cornwall, home of the Museum of Witchcraft, a favorite with both tourists and locals.

Cecil's occult beliefs were reached through diverse paths. He was born in Paignton, Devon. His father was a high-ranking military officer who referred to his son as "the village idiot." The young Williamson did not have a happy childhood. He was looked after by a nanny and often sent to stay with relatives. Some holidays were spent with his uncle, the vicar of North Bovey, in Devon. Here he had his first encounter with witchcraft and persecution.

The gooseberry defense

"One afternoon I had in my mind to toddle off after lunch and scrunch some of Uncle's nice dessert gooseberries, so to the kitchen garden I went. But I quickly realized that there was something going on over the high stone wall in the central green of North Bovey. Dogs were barking, children were squeaking and there was a general hum of conversation, so I went to the garden gate. Sure enough there was something going on. Being an inquisitive little so and so, I hopped across the road and made for the center of things. I arrived just as four burly agricultural types were stripping the last garments, down to complete nudity, of a little old lady who lived quite close to the vicarage. She was absolutely stark naked. I don't know what drove me, there was some impulse, but I pushed my way forward and threw my arms around this naked body lying on the ground and hung on like grim death. I was kicked, I was beaten, I was punched, but I hung on and on and, all of a sudden, everything went dead quiet and a pair of more friendly hands came down and lifted me up. There was Uncle, saying 'Cecil, go back to the vicarage at once.' "

It turned out, according to Cecil, that some of the locals had thought that this old woman was a witch and had set out to prove it by finding a third nipple on her – a sure sign of witchcraft. This incident was the start of a lifelong interest in witchcraft; especially village witchcraft or "wayside witchcraft," as Cecil liked to call it. He loved to tell a good story – some exaggerated or invented – but most are based on fact.

After his schooling Cecil's magical education continued in Rhodesia, where he went to grow tobacco. It was here that he realized that the principles of village witchcraft are universal – the African witch doctors were using similar techniques to English wayside witches. In 1930 Williamson returned to Britain to work in the movie industry, where he met his wife Gwen. His study of the occult was now becoming known and he was exchanging letters and meeting with the country's leading experts, including Wallis Budge of the British Museum, anthropologist Margaret Murray and historian Montague Summers.

British Secret Service

A few years later he was approached by Colonel Maltby of M16, British Secret Service, a friend of Cecil's father. Maltby had heard of the occult interest in Nazi Germany and needed the names of leading military personnel that were practicing the occult. Cecil had become an undercover agent working for MI6. After Cecil's death last year, partner Liz Crow found a hidden room with racks of government files marked "Top Secret." We also found instructions for using a tiny spy camera, also stamped "Top Secret."

Around this time during the thirties Cecil founded the Witchcraft Research Centre and set off for Germany. He

returned with a list of two thousand names of Nazi military personnel dabbling in the occult. Cecil's involvement with MI6 and military mystical research continued through World War II. His occult knowledge was used to lure Rudolf Hess to fly to Scotland.

Enter Gerald Gardner

In 1946 Williamson first met Gerald Gardner in the Atlantis Bookshop, London. Over the next few years they were to become friends and business partners, but the relationship ended in mistrust, fighting and bitterness. The museum archives have a collection of letters from Gardner to Williamson, mainly from the early 1950s, which demonstrate the rise and fall of their relationship.

Williamson purchased the Witches Mill site on the Isle of Man in 1948 and started the massive task of rebuilding and converting it into a museum and restaurant. We know that Gardner was in contact with Williamson throughout the refurbishment process and was constantly advising him on how it should be done. He was also trying to sell Williamson his "witches hut," located on a nudist camp in Brickets Wood, Hertfordshire. According to Williamson, purchase of this hut and the cost of relocating it had put Gardner in a desperate financial position. Gardner apparently turned up at Williamson's museum, suitcase in hand, and pleaded for the job of resident witch! His wish was granted.

Gardner was present at the launch of the museum and was selling signed copies of his new book, *High Magic's Aid*. The text reputedly revealed the rituals of a coven of witches that Gardner had become involved with in the New Forest. This group, the Southern Coven, lent the museum the collection of its working tools and magical items.

Gardner continued to court publicity and succeeded in persuading several newspapers, radio and television journalists to cover witchcraft. He did not like many of the interviews. But the resultant publicity was timely and good for the museum – the coverage coincided with media attention to repeal of the Witch Suppression Act of 1951.

Williamson wanted the museum to show folk magic and the way of the "wayside witch," but knew that the public wanted sensational displays. Gerald did not approve of Cecil's displays and was not at all happy that Cecil removed a photograph of him from the Southern Coven display and had moved some of the objects to different cases.

After this incident Gerald and Cecil did not get on very well and the Southern Coven wrote to Williamson demanding the return of the collection. Stories abound of the feuding between Williamson and Gardner, each of whom seemed to bring out the worst in each other. Williamson even told that Gardner had tried to stab him with his athame.

Thumbs down

Eventually Cecil decided to move his museum back to England. In 1954 he purchased a building near Windsor Castle and moved in his collection. The Witches Mill building was sold to Gardner, who continued to run it as a museum of witchcraft. After Cecil had moved out Gardner's collection was not enough to fill the cases, and he had to borrow many of Williamson's talismans and amulets.

When Gardner died in 1964, the contents of the Isle of Man museum were inherited by Monique Wilson (Lady Olwen), Gardner's high priestess. Williamson asked in vain for the return of his loaned artifacts. Cecil was not a man to be messed with. He placed a curse on the objects " to bring discomfiture to the enemy." Wilson soon sold the complete collection to a museum in America. Years later, when the collection was being broken up and sold, Cecil advised me not to purchase any of these items. I took his advice!

Witchcraft and Windsor were not good partners. Cecil had not been open long when he had a visit from "two grey suited gentleman from the castle." It appeared that the royal family did not approve of Cecil's exhibition on their doorstep; these gentlemen made Cecil a financial offer he couldn't refuse. The Witchcraft Museum was on the move again. With all his expenses being paid by the "men in grey," Cecil moved the collection to the beautiful Cotswold village of Bourton on the Water. The Christian community was not pleased with the arrival of Williamson and his museum. The village priest gave a sermon warning of the evil now amongst

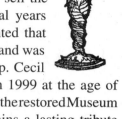

them. This infuriated Cecil, as he was not in a position to answer back. But he did write to the priest and received a copy of the sermon, both documents available in the museum archive. Unfortunately for everyone, two weeks later the priest dropped dead. Cecil does not say that he placed a curse, but he does not say that he didn't.

Brave villagers still held protests outside the museum and ranted about evil and Satanism. Cecil received death threats, fire bombs, had dead cats hung from trees in the garden and eventually an arson attack burned out one wing of the museum.

At home in Cornwall

It was time to move yet again. This time Cecil moved back to his beloved West Country. In 1961 he relocated the Museum of Witchcraft to Boscastle, Cornwall, where it has remained for forty years.

The early years in Boscastle were not without problems. Christians opposed planning permissions, daubed paint over windows and reported the museum to the police for indecency. By now Cecil knew how to handle the ranting of protestors. He ran his museum, kept a low profile and employed staff from the village. Cecil was a good boss and looked after his staff. The museum slowly started receiving donations from the area and Cecil's collection took on a "West Country" feel.

Cecil ran the museum until 1996, when at midnight on October 31 he sold it to me. Cecil was getting on in years and thought it was time to retire. He had been trying to sell the museum for several years and seemed delighted that the collection sold and was not to be broken up. Cecil Williamson died in 1999 at the age of ninety. We hope that the restored Museum of Witchcraft remains a lasting tribute to this remarkable man.

– GRAHAM KING

For a Cecil Williamson Almanac Extra, see www.TheWitchesAlmanac.com/ AlmanacExtras.

The Morrigan

There arose a wild, impetuous, precipitate, mad, inexorable, furious, dark, lacerating, merciless, combative, contentious Badb, which was shrieking and fluttering over their heads; and they were inciting and sustaining valour and battle with them.

— *W. M. Hennessy* on the battle of Clontarf, 1014 C.E.

THE MORRIGAN is the Irish survival of an ancient Gaulish triple mother goddess personifying slaughter and war. Igniting battle frenzy in her chosen warriors, she flies over her enemies and inflicts them with "weakness" in their kidneys. She is also the sorrowful washer at the ford, making the river run with blood as she washes the clothes of those soon to die.

The Morrigu, as she is sometimes called, is also referred to as Morrigan, Badb, Macha and sometimes Nemain, "venomous," or Fea, "the hateful." Agreement may never be reached about whether these names represent separate identities or aspects of one.

Morrigan probably means "Great Queen," which seems more title than name. Her origins probably lie as a guardian of the land's fertility. She characteristically conveys her blessings before battle on Dagda by mating with him in a river in which she washes herself with one foot on each bank.

Another manuscript also recounts the Great Queen of the fairies offering her favors this time to Cuchulain during a battle lull. He spurns her and she reacts by attacking him. When viewed in the Celtic context as a sovereign land goddess choosing her rightful king, her reaction to Cuchulain is easy to interpret.

As a shape shifter, the Morrigan prefers the shape of a crow, but can shift into any form, including an eel, heifer or she-wolf.

Macha, translating to "field" or "plain," prefers the form of a gray horse. Several incarnations of Macha exist in myth, most recounting tales of her death(s) when, in a sense, she is reaped.

In myth, the Badb prefers the form of a carrion crow. Later Irish folklore identifies her with the *bean-sidhe* (banshee), a female family spirit whose wail presages a death in the house.

— Nialla ni Macha

Hot Cross Buns, Sweet Pagans

Hot cross buns, hot cross buns, one a penny, two a penny, hot cross buns.
— Traditional street hawker cry

IT IS A familiar oddity that many customs, myths and foods enjoyed at Christian holidays have their origins in pagan traditions. Traditionally eaten on Good Friday, hot cross buns are thought to predate Christianity. The "hot" in hot cross buns is a relatively new development. Before heating became customary, they were just "cross buns" – buns marked with a frosting of cross. The cross of Christianity had been added as a blessing to protect those who ate them. Many people believed that if they failed to eat a crossed bun on Good Friday ill luck would pursue them throughout the year. The belief in the protective power of the buns, however, predated the cross.

According to nineteenth-century historian Thomas Wright, "The Christians, when they seized upon the Easter festival, gave them the form of a bun, which, indeed, was at that time the ordinary form of bread; and to protect themselves, and those who eat them, from any enchantment, or other evil influences which might arise from their former heathen character, they marked them with the Christian symbol – the cross."

The former "heathen character" of the buns refers to their history as sacred cakes purchased at the entrance to the ancient Temples of Irqata in northern Lebanon. The honey-sweetened consecrated bread would be offered to the gods or eaten for their healing or protective properties. These buns were associated with the celebration of Eostre, a dawn goddess, from whose name we derive the word Easter.

You may wish to celebrate the goddess of spring with an offering of these special buns or to avail yourself of their protective and healing properties. Further your enjoyment with the knowledge that the cross was also considered to represent the four quarters of the moon or the four corners of the earth. The typical hot cross bun is a standard yeast-bun recipe enhanced with spices and currants or raisins; form your own symbolic decoration with the frosting. Whatever the topping, the hot cross bun is a seasonal celebration with an ancient sacred food.

– MORVEN WESTFIELD

Moon Cycles

A New Moon rises with the Sun,
Her waxing half at midday shows,
The Full Moon climbs at sunset hour,
And waning half the midnight knows.

NEW 2011	FULL	NEW 2012	FULL
January 4	January 19	January 23	January 9
February 2	February 18	February 21	February 7
March 4	March 19	March 22	March 8
April 3	April 17	April 21	April 6
May 3	May 17	May 20	May 5
June 1	June 15	June 19	June 4
July 1, 30 (Black Moon)	July 15	July 19	July 3
August 28	August 13	August 17	Aug. 1, 31 (Blue Moon)
September 27	September 12	September 15	September 29
October 26	October 11	October 15	October 29
November 25	November 10	November 13	November 28
December 24	December 10	December 13	December 28

Life takes on added dimension when you
match your activities to the waxing and waning of the Moon.
Observe the sequence of her phases to learn
the wisdom of constant change within complete certainty.

presage

by Dikki-Jo Mullen

ARIES 2010 — PISCES 2011

Almost nothing is the same anymore. The familiar rules once thought to assure a secure and successful future have all dissolved. Does this mean we're on the brink of welcoming a new Golden Age? Or is it a foreshadowing of the End? Since both paths stretch before us as the year begins, true answers emerge from the individual choices made.

This year there are four eclipses, three of them in cardinal signs. There are also three retrograde Mercury cycles through the year and a retrograde Venus during the autumn. Uranus makes a rare sign change, joined by Jupiter in Aries in the springtime, while Saturn wavers on the Virgo–Libra cusp for much of the year. With Pluto in Capricorn, a strong cardinal sign influence is pervasive. Cardinal energy is active and concerned with the present. The emphasis is upon taking care of situations promptly and rejoicing in the here and now.

Explore the sections related to your Sun, Moon, and rising sign (ascendant). The Sun sign reveals where you will shine. It illuminates your life's purpose and defines individuality. It's the single most important factor in the birth chart. The Moon delves into emotional reactions and the needs of everyday life. It reveals the instincts and the influences of heredity. The ascendant relates to physical conditions, your environment, and the body. It shows how others see and react to you.

The daily Moon Calendar is a mainstay in *The Witches' Almanac*, as is traditional in all almanacs. Look at the Moon Calendar, retrogrades and eclipses, the fixed star feature, and the twelve sign overviews to find your way through the year. Keep watch on the heavenly bodies as the year unfolds. Their journeys mirror the coming life experiences each day on this planet, our cyclical home within the cosmos.

ASTROLOGICAL KEYS

Signs of the Zodiac
Channels of Expression

ARIES: fiery, pioneering, competitive
TAURUS: earthy, stable, practical
GEMINI: dual, lively, versatile
CANCER: protective, traditional
LEO: dramatic, flamboyant, warm
VIRGO: conscientious, analytical
LIBRA: refined, fair, sociable
SCORPIO: intense, secretive, ambitious
SAGITTARIUS: friendly, expansive
CAPRICORN: cautious, materialistic
AQUARIUS: inquisitive, unpredictable
PISCES: responsive, dependent, fanciful

Elements
FIRE: Aries, Leo, Sagittarius
EARTH: Taurus, Virgo, Capricorn
AIR: Gemini, Libra, Aquarius
WATER: Cancer, Scorpio, Pisces

Qualities

CARDINAL	FIXED	MUTABLE
Aries	Taurus	Gemini
Cancer	Leo	Virgo
Libra	Scorpio	Sagittarius
Capricorn	Aquarius	Pisces

CARDINAL signs mark the beginning of each new season — active.
FIXED signs represent the season at its height — steadfast.
MUTABLE signs herald a change of season — variable.

Celestial Bodies
Generating Energy of the Cosmos

Sun: birth sign, ego, identity
Moon: emotions, memories, personality
Mercury: communication, intellect, skills
Venus: love, pleasures, the fine arts
Mars: energy, challenges, sports
Jupiter: expansion, religion, happiness
Saturn: responsibility, maturity, realities
Uranus: originality, science, progress
Neptune: dreams, illusions, inspiration
Pluto: rebirth, renewal, resources

Glossary of Aspects

Conjunction: two planets within the same sign or less than 10 degrees apart, favorable or unfavorable according to the nature of the planets.

Sextile: a pleasant, harmonious aspect occurring when two planets are two signs or 60 degrees apart.

Square: a major negative effect resulting when planets are three signs from one another or 90 degrees apart.

Trine: planets four signs or 120 degrees apart, forming a positive and favorable influence.

Quincunx: a mildly negative aspect produced when planets are five signs or 150 degrees apart.

Opposition: a six sign or 180 degrees separation of planets generating positive or negative forces depending on the planets involved.

The Houses — *Twelve Areas of Life*

1st house: appearance, image, identity
2nd house: money, possessions, tools
3rd house: communications, siblings
4th house: family, domesticity, security
5th house: romance, creativity, children
6th house: daily routine, service, health
7th house: marriage, partnerships, union
8th house: passion, death, rebirth, soul
9th house: travel, philosophy, education
10th house: fame, achievement, mastery
11th house: goals, friends, high hopes
12th house: sacrifice, solitude, privacy

Eclipses

Eclipses bring unexpected change. A hint of the specific change brewing comes about ninety days before an eclipse, while its impact unfolds over many months following. When an eclipse takes place within three days of your birthday it augurs a very interesting year. It's imprudent to force issues during an eclipse. Instead, let the universe make the first move, then make a carefully considered response. Upon a return to the light a new perspective, a different interpretation of things, is inevitable. The year ahead brings four eclipses.

June 26, 2010	Full Moon Lunar in Capricorn, north node — partial
July 11, 2010	New Moon Solar in Cancer, south node — total
December 21, 2010	Full Moon Lunar in Gemini, south node — total
January 4, 2011	New Moon Solar in Capricorn, north node — partial

Retrograde Planetary Motion

A retrograde planet seems to trace a backwards course. This optical illusion is created by the planet's speed of travel relative to the Earth's rate of motion. To use the energy of retrograde cycles wisely, reevaluate, retrace, revisit, repeat, or revamp. Seize the opportunity to overcome a mistake or turn a past disappointment into something positive.

Mercury Retrograde Cycles

Three or four times each year for about three weeks, retrograde Mercury delays travel, scrambles appointments, reroutes mail, and brings news from people who have been out of touch. Use this time to tie up loose ends, complete an ongoing project, and travel familiar paths. A residential move or the start of a new job while Mercury is retrograde will lack permanence and stability. Use great caution in making a promise or signing a contract. Retrograde Mercury cycles favor past life regression, planning reunions, and visiting museums, antique shops, and historical sites. Geminis and Virgos feel this influence most of all.

April 18 – May 11, 2010
in Taurus

August 20 – September 12, 2010
in Virgo

December 10 – 30, 2010
in Capricorn and Sagittarius

Venus Retrograde Cycles

Everyone should exercise caution in changing the status of established intimate relationships or finalizing a new commitment during this cycle. It's not at all favorable to marry during retrograde Venus. Venus retrograde affects legal matters, so it's preferable to avoid initiating litigation at this time. Love affairs, social graces, and the fine arts are all complicated by this cycle. Taurus and Libra people are particularly affected by this pattern.

October 8 – November 18, 2010
in Scorpio and Libra

ARIES
The year ahead for those
born under the sign of the Ram
March 20–April 19

Now the bright Sun ascending high,
Dissolves the crystal fields of snow;
A milder luster tints the sky,
While happiness pervades below.

The essence of Aries is perpetually youthful. Restless, forceful, and direct, you are the epitome of the rugged individualist. The head and brain are linked to Aries; those born under this birth sign can be quite intellectual, but also prone to depression and eye strain.

Spring begins on a fair and bright note with Mercury and Venus both in your sign through All Fool's Day. Travel, initiate conversations, socialize, and experiment with artistic expression. Mars remains in Leo, your sister fire sign from early spring until June 7. This is an excellent cycle for assuming leadership roles and focusing on sports or other hobbies. Your energy level is exceptionally high. The New Moon in Aries on April 14 favors setting goals for your birthday and the year to come. Meditate on the direction of your life.

By May Eve Mercury is midway through a retrograde cycle in your finance sector. Examining old experiences and job skills can prove helpful in acquiring greater security. May 21–June 14 Venus enters your home and family sector. A wonderful time begins for interior decorating, acquiring a new home, or dealing in real estate. Family dynamics improve. From Midsummer's Day through July 20 several planets, including Mars, aspect Saturn in your health sector. Release stress and select wholesome foods. Listen to your body. An animal companion may require extra attention.

By Lammastide Jupiter is retrograde in your sign and moves toward an opposition with Saturn. Be aware of how others are influencing you. If a companion generates extra work or worry, back off. Keep your self-confidence high in the face of criticism, excessive competition, or rejection. Learn from it, then move forward. There is a rare, double Full Moon in Aries cycle this year. One lunation is on September 23, the other on October 22. You will be in the spotlight; a long-hidden attribute surfaces. By All Hallows Mars is in Sagittarius where it remains through the first week of December, in favorable aspect to your Sun and the 9th house. Awakening vistas of knowledge bring a renewed sense of freedom.

At Yuletide the Sun, Pluto, and Mars gather in your career sector, aspecting Saturn. Expect shifts in your professional aspirations; a colleague surprises you as the month ends. Welcome change as a necessary catalyst for growth. A legal or ethical issue at work may need attention near the solar eclipse on January 4. The first two weeks of January feature a strong Mercury–Uranus aspect. You'll be impatient. First impressions may change. Even if you eventually regret an impulsive choice, you will learn much. At the same time a favorable trine from Venus is in force. January 8–February 4 social opportunities are bright. A soulmate can appear while you're traveling, exploring a bookstore, or attending a spiritual gathering. This Venusian pattern also favors grandparent–grandchild connections. Since the 9th house is highlighted, plan a memorable dinner at an ethnic restaurant.

By January 23 benevolent Jupiter is in your sign where it remains through winter's end. Your range of opportunity is promising. At Candlemas prepare a collage with pictures of your most extravagant dreams. You'll be pleasantly surprised in months to come at how many of these actually manifest. Throughout February and March, Saturn is retrograde in your 7th house of relationships. Responsibility is a significant element in close partnerships of all kinds. Uranus makes a rare sign change and joins Mercury in Aries by March 12. This planetary combination is brilliant. Innovative solutions to problems are in the wind. The last days of winter are almost electric, hinting at great excitement to come.

HEALTH
April 7–July 21 Saturn, the celestial teacher, is in your 6th house of health. The results of past habits, as well as efforts you've been making to take care of your health, will become apparent then. Since Mercury rules your health sector, travel can often be a wonderful aid to your well-being. You thrive when variety and change surround you. Visit a health spa or try an ocean voyage. A pilgrimage or a quiet visit to a sacred site can stimulate a healing too.

LOVE
Mars adds heat to your 5th house of romance from the vernal equinox through the first week of June. Expect a fiery attraction then. You always enjoy a challenge. Since proud Leo rules your love sector you insist upon quality in romance and appreciate someone who is truly gifted and exceptional. September and October can stir love connections with the two Full Moons in your sign.

SPIRITUALITY
It has been 84 years since Uranus transited Aries. In the late winter Uranus enters your sign where it conjoins your Sun. This heralds a 7-year cycle of all that is fresh and progressive. Sudden changes in outlook are about to impact your spiritual path. As Uranus rules astrology, exploring astrology from a spiritual perspective would be beneficial. The Red Hawk is your shamanic animal guide. A courageous hunter, this beautiful bird soars to great heights to observe the entire situation before moving rapidly to its goal.

FINANCE
Jupiter, the planet of affluence, leaves the 12th house of sacrifice this year. Long-term financial obligations to others near completion. The July and January eclipses affect your domestic and career sectors. Jupiter is about to conjoin your Sun, revealing personal ambition coupled with the opportunity to acquire greater financial acumen. A strong cardinal sign influence suggests some terrific ideas for financial planning and new earning potentials. Follow through. Attention to details will bring on success as the winter ends.

TAURUS
The year ahead for those
born under the sign of the Bull
April 20–May 20

*Earth with landscapes
bright as morning,
Just emerged from winter's gloom,
Hears at length the joyful warning,
And awakes from nature's tomb.*

Ruled by Venus, Taureans often have wonderful artistic skill. Since this birth sign relates to the throat and ears, many fine musicians, especially vocalists, are born in late April or May. Loyal and sincere, you provide comfort and healing to others. There is a deep awareness of the material world and appreciation for harmonious, comfortable surroundings.

Time spent alone is appealing during the earliest days of spring. The Sun joins Mercury and Venus in your 12th house until April 1. There is much going on within that you will keep private. During most of April, Venus glides through your sign while making a grand trine in earth signs. This is extremely promising for financial gain and for enjoying a deep link to planet Earth. April is an optimum time for planting a garden.

From the beginning of spring through the first week of June Mars activates your home and family sector. Home improvements and resolving psychological issues related to family dynamics are priorities. Mercury makes a long passage through Taurus April 11–June 10, including a retrograde cycle. Travel, especially to revisit an old haunt, is very likely. It's also a perfect time to review studies or explore a favorite subject in greater detail. Your persuasive skills are excellent now. The New Moon in Taurus on April 14 brings the specifics into focus.

Near May Day a Saturn–Uranus opposition affects your 5th house of romance. There can be a turning point in a relationship. Accept others as they are or loosen a bond and move forward. When Saturn completes its retrograde as May ends, you'll realize you've outgrown a situation. From the last three weeks of June until just before Lammas a strong Mars transit favorably aspects your Sun. A hobby becomes more important, and a love interest adds excitement to your summer. During August a stellium of Libra planets, including Saturn, gathers in your 6th house. Health and fitness concerns are underscored. This is a great time to add Feng Shui cures to your residence or workplace. An animal companion soothes stress.

During the first two weeks of September retrograde Mercury in your 5th house can re-ignite an old flame. There is better mental rapport with loved ones. Shortly before the autumnal equinox Mars enters your 7th house, remaining there in opposition to your Sun until October 28. Don't make sudden choices regarding partnerships and commitments. Allow others to take the lead. A competitive mood prevails. Have a peaceful, traditional Samhain celebration. Your ruler, Venus, is retrograde during October and early November, favoring past life regression.

On November 21 the Full Moon in your sign finds you more upbeat and enthused overall. From December 8 through mid-January Mars joins Pluto and (for a time) Mercury in your 9th house of spirituality and philosophy. Light real bayberry candles at Yule to assure a healthy, prosperous year ahead. A winter journey can be quite inspirational.

From January 16 to late February Neptune in your career sector is activated by several Aquarius transits. There can be some added stress, illusion, and confusion surrounding career situations. Remember that there are two sides to every story. A dream can bring guidance concerning this near the New Moon on Chinese New Year, February 2. As March begins, Venus crosses your midheaven and makes a favorable aspect to Saturn in your 6th house. This promises more goodwill and a greater sense of security regarding your work. During winter's last days Uranus joins Jupiter in your 12th house. You'll feel a deep compassion for wildlife and be drawn toward forests and fields.

HEALTH

Your Taurus sun sign and your 6th house of health are both linked to Venus. Sweet, rich foods can be quite tempting; enjoy them in moderation. On July 21 Saturn begins a passage which will last several years through your health sector. Hereditary health factors, past patterns, and the health of your daily environment can impact wellness. Patience and good habits will guide you along the path of well-being.

LOVE

Venus spends a very long time in Scorpio, your opposing sign and the 7th house of partnerships, from late summer until early January. During part of this cycle, October 9 – November 19, Venus will be retrograde. A sense of déjà vu tinges relationships, for better or worse. A very charming, attractive person can touch your heart, but keep perspective concerning the situation. April and February bring light, bright love stars your way.

SPIRITUALITY

Pluto is making a very lengthy passage in Capricorn, your 9th house of philosophy and spirituality. Eclipses also affect this sector on June 26 and January 4. Completely new spiritual directions can emerge. A longtime guru can either leave your circle or disappoint you. Look for answers from within regarding a new spiritual group. You might visit several before finding one that resonates. Beaver, the industrious builder of the animal community, is your shamanic guide.

FINANCE

The Gemini eclipse on December 21 affects your financial sector. Taurus resists changes of employment and income streams more than most. However, this pattern makes change almost inevitable. Be receptive to new working conditions or sources of income. Seek opportunities to add to savings while Saturn is favorable April 8–July 20. Dedicate a green crystal, such as jade or emerald, to financial security at the summer solstice.

GEMINI
The year ahead for those
born under the sign of the Twins
May 21–June 20

Now fairy visions flit around
Earth in splendor listens mute,
While the gardener tills the ground
And lives in hopes to reap the fruit.

Articulate and witty, your quick mind reveals that Mercury is your ruler. Your emblem, the Twins, illustrates the duality and versatility which are part of your character. The hands and arms are linked to Gemini, showing innate dexterity. Creative expression using pens, paintbrushes, keyboards, or precision instruments comes easily.

At the vernal equinox a stellium of transits highlights your 11th house. Group activities, humanitarian causes and friendship have great appeal now. On April 7 Saturn enters your 4th house where it remains until July 21. Getting family matters settled, securing your residence, and understanding how hereditary factors influence your current situation will share focus. At the end of April Mercury turns retrograde in your 12th house, going direct on May 11. Memories and dreams are vivid. Mercury remains in Taurus during all of May through June 10. Habits, whether positive or not, will be an important factor. Break away from any negative ideas. Thought forms grow

very real at this time of the cycle.

The Gemini New Moon on June 12 ushers in a time of greater self-confidence. Neptune favorably aspects the lunation, so expect flashes of keen intuition, opportunities for travel, and the exchange of useful ideas with others. Summer begins with Jupiter and Uranus in a sextile aspect, impacting your sector of future goals. Contemporary trends, the pioneer spirit, and intriguing acquaintances inspire you as July begins. The July 11 eclipse in your 2nd house of finances encourages you to embrace new values and consider alternative sources of income.

During August Venus joins Mars and Saturn in your 5th house of romance and recreation. A new love, whether romantic or the love of a new avocation or creative project, adds joy to late summer. September begins with retrograde Mercury and the Sun in Virgo while Uranus is on a critical degree in Pisces. All three placements are in an irritating square aspect to you. Release stress; prepare to juggle home and work responsibilities. Your efforts are appreciated, and you'll make progress by the Full Moon of September 23. During most of October Mercury moves rapidly through Libra, your sister air sign. This enhances communication with loved ones and adds an awareness of beauty and culture. November 8–29 Venus stations and completes its retrograde in your romance sector. A karmic situation regarding loved ones is resolved. You have recently learned a great deal about love. Thanksgiving brings the dual blessings of gratitude and forgiveness.

December begins with Mars in your

opposing sign of Sagittarius. Others can motivate you, but there's a competitive spirit afoot. Use strategy and diplomacy with difficult individuals. The Gemini Full Moon on December 21 is also a total eclipse. Changes and surprises are assured in the months to come. Receptivity is a perfect winter solstice meditation focus. From early January through Candlemas Venus dances through your 7th house of relationships. Celebrate the success of a partner. A very talented, attractive person draws closer to you. It's a favorable time for the resolution of legal matters. February 4–21 Mercury forms a series of positive aspects to air sign planets. Work is more rewarding; you have deeper insight and peace of mind. Learning and travel opportunities are plentiful.

By February 23 Mars joins Uranus in your 10th house. If you rise to the occasion with enthusiasm, this can lead to a professional breakthrough. You are the center of attention. Project the best image possible by making the most of your appearance and by being kind and attentive toward others. As winter wanes there is a very strong accent on the cardinal signs, with Pluto prominent by aspect. Be aware of health factors; get organized. There are situations which must be addressed. Pay immediate attention to present needs.

HEALTH
The June 26 eclipse conjoins Pluto in Capricorn in your 6th house of health. There can be a sudden health need to address, perhaps related to the mouth and teeth. At the end of winter Uranus changes signs, possibly making you vulnerable to contagious colds or flu. If you must be near those who are ill, fashion a nosegay of mint and chamomile and add a blue ribbon for healing. Keep warm and dry in bad weather.

LOVE
On April 25 Venus enters your sign where it remains until May 19. Bless a tall, red pillar candle with rose or vanilla oil to dedicate it to love. Ignite it in the evenings while concentrating on revelry and companionship. You may see results as the Full Moon rises in Scorpio on April 28. When Saturn enters Libra at the end of July, a two-year cycle of stability and commitment regarding love begins. You have an opportunity to build a sincere, lasting relationship.

SPIRITUALITY
Uranus rules your 9th house of spirituality. This unpredictable wanderer makes a rare sign change in the late winter, revealing that you are becoming restless with familiar spiritual pursuits. Your shamanic guide, a Native American totem, is the Deer. Embrace this graceful, elusive creature to draw upon the magic of responsiveness, observation, and flight.

FINANCE
The July 11 solar eclipse affects your financial sector. Be flexible concerning changes in your source of income. A new position or alternative employment may become available. The days each month when the Moon is in an air sign (Gemini, Libra or Aquarius) should be promising regarding finances. Relatives might either offer employment or help you to find income opportunities.

CANCER
The year ahead for those
born under the sign of the Crab
June 21–July 22

The Sun in all bright splendor rife,
In Northern climates brightly reigns;
And marks how all things move in life,
In yonder glowing verdant plains.

Receptive and naturally empathetic, Cancer is very impressionable. You absorb the moods of people around you, so cultivate cheerful associates. You honor promises and get things done, but have a pervasive restlessness. The stomach is linked to this birth sign; Moon children must eat light, healthy meals to avoid digestive upsets.

Spring brings a surge of energy poured into acquiring greater financial security. Mars highlights your 2nd house of money where it remains until June 7. This promises enthusiasm and motivation, but quell anger and impatience regarding finances. Just after All Fool's Day Mercury and Venus brighten the 11th house, forming a sextile aspect to your Sun. Throughout April friendships strengthen. Your creative ideas help make wishes a reality. At Beltane charitable work enriches daily life. Throughout the retrograde Mercury of April 19–May 12 reconnecting with an out-of-touch friend brings peace of mind about a past issue. Late May–June 14 Venus moves through your sign. Relationships of all kinds are happier. It's a great cycle for creative projects or business ventures. Others delight in your company.

The wind of change blows in with the summer solstice and your birthday. An eclipse pattern marks late June through mid-July. Adapt, explore— it's important to realize what must be released. Partnerships of all kinds are in transition. June 25–July 9 Mercury races through your sign. Travel, conversation, and writing are favored. Act quickly for best results. Jupiter and Uranus conjoin in your 10th house during July. Changes involving people and career circumstances bring a new perspective on professional aspirations.

By Lammas Eve Mars joins Saturn in Libra making a square aspect involving the 4th house. Your residence might need repair work. A relative can seek assistance. Take care of one issue at a time. Patience and persistence will pay off. The pressure lessens during September when planetary transits leave the cardinal signs. By Mabon Venus and Mars are in Scorpio, creating very positive influences in your 5th house. The autumn favors romance, connections with children, and taking time to enjoy a hobby. All Hallows finds Mercury trine your Sun, bringing insights and good decision-making ability through early November. On November 18 Jupiter turns direct in Pisces and teams with Uranus in your 9th house through Yuletide, supporting spiritual discovery through study or a pilgrimage.

January opens with a solar eclipse opposing you on the 4th. Expect surprise announcements from others. Double-check rules and regulations of all kinds. On January 15 Mars changes signs, relieving much of the pressure you've been under. Others will be more cooperative by Candlemas. The Full Moon in Cancer on January 19 brings a renewed sense of your own potentials and goals. While basking under the Moon's rays, focus on the famous axiom from the Oracle of Delphi "know thyself."

Throughout February, Jupiter and Pluto form a very strong aspect pattern in cardinal signs. Changing economic conditions and weather can impact both career and closest relationships. Preserve dignity; treasure your honor and reputation. Truth will prevail. A retrograde Saturn in Libra forms favorable aspects to Aquarius transits throughout February and March. It's a wonderful influence for exploring genealogy, making a family scrapbook, or adding to collectibles. February 24–March 9 the Sun, Mercury, Uranus, and Mars form a favorable stellium in Pisces, bringing a higher consciousness. Philosophical and educational pursuits are rewarding. Writing, language studies, and travel are all favored. Winter's last days find Uranus entering Aries. Sudden new opportunities are developing at work. Be very progressive. Invest effort in creating a good impression.

HEALTH
The Full Moon on May 27 impacts your 6th house of health. The four weeks following that lunation can bring a turn for the better regarding fitness. Through January 22 Jupiter's influence provides opportunities to conquer health factors and develop your strength. During the mid and late winter be careful not to go to extremes regarding rich cuisine, overly demanding schedules at work, or exercise sessions. Moderation is the key to optimum health.

LOVE
Eclipses in your 7th house of partnership in June and January promise a year of great change. Either an existing relationship will move in a different direction or an established bond will dissolve to make way for a new attachment. When in doubt, wait and watch. Allow time to reveal what is most conducive to happiness. Cultivate love connections late May–mid-June, September 8–November 7, and November 30–January 7.

SPIRITUALITY
A Uranus influence indicates that you've recently been through a cycle of great spiritual awakening. Now is the time to become more committed to the tradition which has proven most suitable. The Pisces Full Moon on August 24 favors your spiritual quest. Near that date connect with your shamanic animal guide, the Brown Flicker. This beloved bird builds strong nests which, when abandoned, offer other birds or small animals shelter.

FINANCE
March 20–June 6 and again September 9–January 22 a favorable Jupiter aspect provides opportunities to get finances in order. Live within your means and save. This will leave you with a nest egg at the end of winter when there can be some added expenses to deal with. The Sun rules your financial sector. This brings bright prospects if you're an early bird. Be early for deadlines and take care of financial matters during the morning hours to enhance financial security.

LEO
The year ahead for those
born under the sign of the Lion
July 23–August 22

Hark thunder roar let lightning glare,
And the whirlwind sweep along;
All around is pure and fair,
The loved wild birds chant in song.

Courageous, faithful, and loyal, a sunny combination of drama and dignity characterizes Leo. Your charismatic ability to shine often inspires others. The heart and spine are ruled by Leo. You literally pour your heart into all that you do. A backache can be a signal to examine the structure and solidity of your life.

Mars marches into your sign with the vernal equinox, where it remains through the first week of June. Expect an active and challenging time. Much can be accomplished if you don't allow anger or impatience to get the best of you. Get organized, then make your best effort toward an important goal. March 20–31 finds Venus favorably aspecting Mars. Love and artistic projects are slated for success. Mercury makes a long passage through your 10th house April 2–June 10. You may feel uncertain about a career situation. Get the facts straight; misinformation is afoot. Travel and study help you advance. Near Beltane your 11th house is favorable. Keep love friendly and lighthearted; your entire social circle is widening.

Acquaintances who enter your life in early May will remain true friends for a very long while. Community activities, perhaps politics, play a role in this.

Mid-June through mid-July Venus moves rapidly through your sign. One of the very best cycles for love commences. During the last half of July, Mercury in Leo aspects the Aries transits of Uranus and Jupiter, adding sparkle to travel and study. Your witty ways win you admiration and support. By Lammastide Saturn leaves your financial sector where it has created challenges for several years. Near your birthday you enter a phase when you'll feel more secure regarding money. The New Moon in Leo on August 9 favors working with prosperity affirmations. During September Venus begins a long passage through your sector of home and family life. Real estate transactions are favorable through early January. Turn your dwelling into your dream home. Family dynamics improve.

During the first three weeks of October your 3rd house sets the pace. Several placements, including Saturn, sextile your Sun. Relationships with a neighbor or sibling are upbeat and can be a source of valuable ideas. Numerous short outings are in the stars; get organized to keep your schedule free of conflicts. Just before Samhain Mars enters your love and pleasure sector, bestowing happiness and excitement through December 7. Your vitality is excellent as autumn progresses.

The Yuletide eclipse of December 21 finds your goals changing. A friend may need a healing. A very favorable Venus influence builds momentum during the last three weeks of January and culminates just after Candlemas. A loved one enjoys exceptional success. You'll take pleasure in creative work or hobbies. An avocation could be a source of extra income. The February 18 Full Moon in Leo brings a hint of nostalgia. A meditation on that lunation enhances self understanding. Visualize personal success. During the remainder of February cadent house influences are strong. Plans for the future have a subtle, even furtive tone. There is much going on beneath the surface. Your mindset creates your world. Let your thoughts weave a haven, not a Hades.

On March 1 Venus joins Neptune in Aquarius, your opposing sign. This applying conjunction lasts through the end of the month. Those closest to you are elusive and dreamy. Be tolerant if a dear one shows eclectic preferences in fashion, art, or entertainment. Double-check the details if legal issues need attention. The New Moon on March 4 accents the 8th house. Seek a solution to a mystery. Your insight is keen. Hypnosis, especially past life regression, can be very successful as winter fades into spring.

HEALTH
Eclipses on June 26 and January 4 in your health sector conjoin Pluto. Prepare for some changes in your vitality. Since Pluto has a relationship to crowds and mass karma, take precautions to keep a distance from those who appear unwell. If a large crowd gathers in an area where inclement weather or other troublesome environmental factors are present, protect personal well-being and comfort. Brew fresh sage leaves as a tea or add some to a hearty soup. Burn a sage smudge to drive away any ills.

LOVE
Neptune, which has been in your sector of relationships for many years, turns retrograde June 3–November 10. It promises a sensitivity to patterns with loved ones as well as past life links which impact relationships. From the first week of September through the first week of January Venus brightens your domestic environment. Time spent in the privacy of homey surroundings will foster love.

SPIRITUALITY
The September and October Full Moons are in Aries, which rules your 9th house of spirituality. This suggests a spiritual awakening before the autumn has passed. New concepts in spirituality, perhaps involving the unleashing of the kundalini, are about to impact you. The Sturgeon is an animal guide you can connect with for a shamanic experience. This fish has a legendary ability to bluff its way out of any difficulties.

FINANCE
A difficult Saturn transit in your 2nd house of finances has created some frustration in recent years. A more promising cycle begins near your birthday. Welcome it by preparing a prosperity ritual for Lammastide. Light a green candle, encircle it with cinnamon powder. When the candle is gone, gather some of the cinnamon to scatter near your doorway and in your shoes. Jupiter, the celestial benefactor, trines your Sun in late winter and should replenish your coffers.

VIRGO
The year ahead for those
born under the sign of the Virgin
August 23-September 22

Zephyrs gentle and regaling,
Wave the fields of yellow grain;
As summer's heat's prevailing,
Cool the parched and sunlit plain.

Discriminating and methodical, your quiet reserve and common sense inspire the trust of others. Analytical, with excellent communication skills, teaching, media work, and medicine are interests which captivate you. The lower digestive tract and nervous system are linked to Virgo. Proper elimination and stress control are always important. The Virgin, your emblem, hints at a certain inner purity of purpose.

At the vernal equinox Mars enters your 12th house where it remains through the first week of June. Plans for the future stir within you, but it isn't easy to implement action. A needy person makes demands. Offer help to the extent that you sense appreciation, but don't allow another to drain your time or resources. During most of April Venus forms a bright trine involving your 9th house. Music and art can heighten spiritual experiences. Relationships with in-laws, grandparents, and grandchildren enrich your life.

May 1-12 favorable earth sign transits impact you. A healing perspective on loss builds momentum. Communicate with someone who attracts you. Perform a May Eve blessing dedicated to the future of an important love connection. Mars races through your sign and shadows Saturn June 8–July 29, lending an assertive, competitive note to all that you do. Combine this valuable motivation with a dash of patience and a goal can be reached. Older people and traditions offer valuable insight. The best gift you can give yourself during early summer is a few extra hours of rest. A fresh apple is better than caffeine for a pick-me-up if you feel tired. Channel any feelings of anger or resentment into constructive outlets of expression. Exercise is wonderful, but remember to use moderation and have cool drinks nearby if you're active outdoors.

From mid-July to August 6, Venus blesses your sign, heralding a memorable cycle for love and pleasure. Plan a vacation, pursue a hobby, and cultivate romance. During all of August and September until October 3 Mercury makes a very long, intense passage through Virgo. This ushers in restlessness, heightened awareness, and curiosity. Travel and educational activities bring deep satisfaction. It's the ideal time to complete a writing project. The stars favor efforts to publish everything—fiction, nonfiction, prose, or poetry. October finds your 2nd house of finances affected by a combination of the Sun, Mercury, and Saturn. Appreciate what you have; seek bargains on big ticket items. Patience, creative expression, and the encouragement of friends all have a positive impact on security concerns during this time.

On October 7 the New Moon conjoins 2nd house transits. Bless a tiny green jade Buddha or a pendant fashioned of iron pyrite for financial success then. By Samhain Mars aspects your home and family sector, an influence which lasts through the first week of December. A relative is assertive. Home improvement projects have appeal. Eliminate potential safety hazards promptly. Near Yuletide Jupiter conjoins Uranus in your 7th house of partnerships. Relationships are in flux. Someone close to you has a surprise to share. Study this person's eyes and facial expressions for best response.

January 1–15 Capricorn transits, including Mars and Pluto, add new intensity to your love life. Past life connections can be evident. It's a passionate cycle. This passion can manifest in artistic endeavors, in perfecting ability in a sport, or in romance. In late January Jupiter enters Aries to highlight your 8th house. New options regarding business and investments are presented. Insurance or tax situations turn in your favor. Just after Candlemas dream symbols reveal subtle clues regarding health care. March 1–19 Venus transits your health sector. Seek the perfect health care practitioner. Healing of both body and spirit occurs. The first half of March brings stimulating conversations, as Mercury opposes your Sun. Draw down the Virgo Full Moon on March 19. Give thanks for the times past and honor completion at moonrise.

HEALTH
Elusive, mystical Neptune is in the final year of a long passage through your health sector. It's time to let go of what hasn't worked well and embrace what has. Dream interpretation and visualization can help you approach wellness goals. This is especially true near the time of the Full Moon of July 25 and again during the winter months.

LOVE
Two eclipses, on June 26 and January 24, fall in your 5th house of love. Both are near Pluto. This promises an intense cycle regarding the search for love. Endings followed by new beginnings are likely. Karmic conditions come into play. Consider regressive hypnosis if the love situation is too complex. During April, July, and near Valentine's Day Venus transits earth signs creating fertile ground for seeds of love.

SPIRITUALITY
The Brown Bear spirit is a shamanic animal closely linked to your birth sign. The Bear hibernates, revealing that plenty of sleep is essential to your spiritual health. The New Moon on May 13 and the Full Moon on November 21 are in Taurus, your 9th house of spirituality. Devote those dates to spirituality.

FINANCE
Saturn leaves your sign and begins a two-year passage through your 2nd house of finances. Patience is important. Above all, live within your means; gradual but steady gains are on the way. Update your salable job skills or learn how to generate a new source of income. Realistic effort will pay off. During May a grand trine in earth signs promises more ease in monetary matters. Follow through with financial opportunities in the springtime.

LIBRA
The year ahead for those
born under the sign of the Scales
September 23–October 23

Hand around the nectar cup,
Nature yield the precious balm.
Drink the sparkling contents up,
This is pleasant, mild and calm.

Refined, realistic, and sociable, Librans seek balance. Relationships and finding happiness through compromise are always important. You enjoy being surrounded by comfort and beauty. The lower back and kidneys are linked to your sign. Try massage to stimulate and relax that area of the body. Drinking plenty of fresh water and juices helps your general well-being.

Early spring brings a temporary respite from challenges. Saturn is retrograde, leaving your sign. It retreats completely by April 8. The Libra Full Moon of March 29 accents many oppositions in the heavens. Create harmony with aromatherapy and music. During most of April Mercury and Venus activate the 8th house. Others can impact your finances; research helps you make the wisest choices. During May Venus is in Gemini, moving toward a trine with Neptune in Aquarius. This very romantic and creative influence sheds harmony on you. It culminates May 18–19. Share dreams, amusements and pleasures with the one you love most.

Late May through June 7 Mars brings dynamic and adventurous friends into your social circle. Early June finds Jupiter joining Uranus in Aries where they hover in a conjunction until August 13, impacting the cusp of your 7th house. Partnerships grow in new directions. Be an exceptionally good listener now. The eclipse on June 26 relates directly to domestic situations. Since it involves Pluto, there can be new developments involving your family or neighborhood as a whole. The solar eclipse of July 11 points to new career horizons. By Lammastide the specifics will be revealed. At the early harvest set aside what you'll need for the future. Conserve and all will be well.

Throughout August until September 13 Mars moves through Libra, gifting you with energy and enthusiasm. Quell anger and impatience and much can be accomplished. This is a wonderful influence for developing a daily yoga practice or improving your tennis game. As Mabon nears, your 2nd house is highlighted. Seek opportunities to add to your earnings. On October 7, when the Moon is new in Libra, meditate on your birthday goals. Write affirmations for the year to come. October 4-20 Mercury races past a conjunction with your Sun. This is wonderful for travel, and you'll communicate well.

By Samhain Saturn will be lumbering steadily along, intent on its two-year passage over your Sun. The use of time, recognizing parameters, the satisfaction of fulfilling responsibilities are all positive ways to make the best of this. December 1–January 7 amicable Venus affects your financial sector. A friend helps with recommendations or offers related to security. Your creativity may add to your income as well. The January 4 eclipse links to a stellium of planets, including Mars and Pluto, in your home and family sector all month, heralding a new phase in family life. A surprise surfaces regarding your heritage. Sorting through family keepsakes and photos can be a part of this.

On Candlemas your 5th house of love and romance is brightened by the Sun and Mars, with Mercury following on February 4. The Full Moon on February 18 brightens the way to selecting worthwhile goals. It's a good time to commit to a service organization or accept a volunteer position. Diplomatically release those associations which you've outgrown. The end of February finds a series of four Pisces transits moving through your 6th house, the health sector. Gather information about exercise and diet; recognize the connection between mindset and physical wellness. Getting organized and enjoying an animal companion can help to release anxiety. On March 12 Uranus joins Jupiter in Aries, your opposing sign. This promises excitement through unpredictable people at winter's end. Check with your inner compass about offbeat suggestions and activities.

HEALTH
Jupiter, the celestial physician and problem solver, moves through your health sector March 20–June 6 and again September 10–January 22. Seek relief from chronic conditions then. Change your lifestyle for the better during these times and your health can be favorably affected for many years to come. Uranus is just completing a long passage

through Pisces, the last zodiac sign and ruler of the feet. This has a tie to health in your horoscope. It also symbolizes the importance of proper foot care and an end to a phase regarding ailments.

LOVE
The Venus retrograde of October 9–November 19 can bring powerful reincarnation associations about love into focus. Visit a place related to a past life memory to better understand the promise of love. The New Moon on February 2 is the start of the Chinese Year of the Rabbit. For you, it's exceptionally favorable for love. Invoke the favor of the Rabbit with a New Year party.

SPIRITUALITY
Mercury rules your 9th house of spirituality. The three retrograde Mercury cycles this year are wonderful times to detach from the tangible world and explore spiritual potentials. The December 21 eclipse in Gemini affects your spirituality. A winter solstice message will open new avenues of perception. The Raven is your shamanic animal guide, admired for its communication gifts.

FINANCE
The eclipse of July 11 on your midheaven accents new situations regarding your status. Since the Moon phases rule your 10th house of fame and fortune, always seek promotions using the lunar signs and phases as a guide. Lunar-ruled symbols and crystals can be effective talismans for worldly success. Saturn begins a long passage through your sign this year. Patiently hang in there and keep trying. Eventually the rewards will come.

SCORPIO
The year ahead for those
born under the sign of the Scorpion
October 24–November 21

Lovely autumn, how delicious,
Flow in grief or melt in sorrow,
Grapes in ripening clusters precious,
Cheer today and gild tomorrow.

Purposeful, ambitious, and subtle with an enormous ability to heal and transform, Scorpios are co-ruled by Mars and Pluto. This emotional water sign has hidden depths. You harbor feelings with great intensity. Physiologically, the reproductive system is linked to Scorpio. Creativity and deep passions affect both physical and mental health.

Spring introduces a competitive note regarding career. Mars is square your Sun and accidentally exalted while highlighting your 10th house of fortune and fame until early June. Keep rivalry good-natured to assure advancement. Near All Fool's Day Venus enters your relationship sector where it remains until April 25. Be supportive when a partner has success. A charming, talented person feels drawn to you. On April 28 the Full Moon falls in Scorpio, ushering in a four-week cycle of excitement. You have many opportunities to show your talents. The right people will take note.

Throughout May until June 10 Mercury is volatile. Expect some conflicts. Allow others to express opposing view-points. Have a back-up plan if someone doesn't follow through on a commitment. Jupiter enters your health sector in mid-June, and a cycle of recovery commences. Relief is found for both physical and emotional ills as Midsummer's Day nears. The eclipses of June 26 and July 11 affect your 3rd and 9th houses, respectively. Impromptu travel plans can develop; you'll also be drawn to learning. By August both Mars and Saturn are in your 12th house. Take time for quiet reflection. Much is taking place on the subconscious level. You'd find great solace through getting involved in charity work.

By September 9 Venus begins a long passage through your sign which lasts through November 7, then repeats November 30–January 7. Love is about to take a dramatic turn for the better. An old flame might re-ignite and burn with renewed ardor. You might also heal from a past disappointment. New happiness in matters of the heart is nearby, waiting to be discovered. Be receptive. October 21–November 7 a favorable Mercury trend brings intellectual strength. Answers to dilemmas come; travel opportunities are rewarding. Near your birthday Neptune completes a retrograde and squares your sign. There is much illusion afoot. Sift through it patiently to discover what is real.

Late November through mid-December your 2nd house of money is accented by Mars, then the Sun. You'll pour extra effort into attaining financial security. Seek the best price on expensive items; postpone luxury purchases and add to your nest egg instead. The winter solstice eclipse on December 21 opens the gates to the afterlife, for it falls in your 8th house. A connection with the spirit world offers insight and comfort. This link can continue to grow throughout the year ahead if you're receptive. Late December–January 13 Mercury hovers in your money sector. It's a wonderful time to explore new sources of income and make decisions about purchases. A journey or a conversation can have a positive impact on finances.

Mid-January through February 22 a series of transits in Aquarius affects your 4th house. An agitated relative may need encouragement. Residential repairs or a real estate transaction can be considered. The New Moon on February 2 reveals the specifics. Mars, Mercury, and the Sun join Uranus in your 5th house of love from late February through the first part of March. A new love interest is afoot. A creative project or avocation motivates you. Honor the source of your passion to find renewed meaning in life. After March 12 Uranus joins Jupiter in your 6th house. Daily routine can be disrupted during the last days of winter. Connections with domestic and wild animals will intensify. A relationship with a beloved pet can deepen and become richer.

HEALTH

A powerful, unusual conjunction involving Jupiter and Uranus hovers near the cusp of your health sector most of the year, until finally both planets enter completely during the winter season. Stress must be controlled. Alternative treatments can lead to healing. Be aware of changes involving health. Temperature extremes and other environmental factors can affect well-being. Invest in comfortable clothing.

LOVE

A seven-year cycle of erratic love situations gives way to a time of greater stability. You are deeply affected by attachments and have had difficulty releasing unsatisfactory bonds. Venus makes a long retrograde, spending most of the time in Scorpio, from early September until early January. An autumn and winter romance brings happiness. Keep things light near Halloween, when Venus is retrograde. Past patterns in love are operative. Repeat only the good ones. Accept and issue invitations at Mabon and Yule. These times show great potential for true happiness.

SPIRITUALITY

The total solar eclipse of July 11 sextiles Mars, your co-ruler, and deeply affects your 9th house of spirituality. Connections with friends or networking within an organization will likely impact your changing spiritual perceptions all year. Time spent near water, an aquarium, a shell collection, and recordings of ocean sounds can all heighten spiritual perceptions. The Serpent, a symbol of wisdom, the rising kundalini, and eternal life, is your shamanic animal guide during this significant time.

FINANCE

Benevolent Jupiter trines your Sun from the vernal equinox through June 6 and again September 9–January 22. Financial prospects are promising during those months. Implement creative ideas and explore ways enjoyable activities can generate income. Try new avenues in seeking financial security. A calculated risk or educated guess can pay off handsomely now.

SAGITTARIUS
The year ahead for those
born under the sign of the Archer
November 22–December 21

Stripped of all their recent splendor
Are the trees of yonder wood;
Thus all nature must surrender,
And confess the change is good.

Uninhibited, you thrive on freedom and play every game to win. Your intuition is excellent, and you express your opinions candidly, sometimes coming across as rather blunt. Sagittarians have an affinity for pets of all kinds, especially horses and large dogs. Look to blood sugar levels, the liver, and thigh area for the source of health considerations.

The vernal equinox has a fiery quality with Mars in Leo and the Aries Sun forming trines to your Sun. An adventurous spirit is present and you can make exciting plans for travel and study. Your energy level is at a peak through the first week of June. Romantic prospects are wonderful through All Fool's Day, as Venus brightens your 5th house of love and pleasure. Mercury makes a long passage through your 6th house of health April 3–June 10. Gather information about health, diet, and healthcare options. It's an excellent cycle for visualizing and affirming wellness. Your ability to communicate with animal friends is in top form most of the spring; you can forge a deeper bond with them.

A lost animal returns while Mercury is retrograde April 19–May 12.

Draw down the Full Moon in Sagittarius on May 27. It ushers in a hectic month. Prioritize and much can be accomplished. June 15–July 10 Venus transits Leo. It's a perfect cycle for vacation travel and enjoying mystical art and music. The eclipse of July 11 in your 8th house brings secrets to light. Accept the inevitable. Be leery of financial advice and deals offered by others. On July 24 Jupiter, your ruler, turns retrograde. This lasts through November 19. Ongoing dwelling and family issues need attention. A relative requires your care and encouragement.

By Lammastide Mercury creates a stir, as it makes a long passage through your 10th house of career, culminating on October 3. New elements affect your vocation. Be observant, remain willing to learn, and all will be well. Saturn enters your 11th house during the summer, where it will remain for two years. Throughout August Mars conjoins Saturn, bringing added emphasis to its lessons. Worthwhile goals lay the foundation for your long-term future. Be very careful to keep good company. Connect with admirable associates. Release negative individuals.

At the autumnal equinox your 12th house is accented by Venus in Scorpio. Dreams bring you significant messages about love near each of the rare double Full Moons in Aries on September 23 and October 22. During the weeks leading up to Samhain you'll cherish solitary moments. During all of November through December 7 Mars moves through Sagittarius, making you a bit edgy and even more abrupt than usual.

However, it also enhances motivation. Get organized, make an extra effort. Personal goals can be reached.

During December Capricorn planets in your 2nd house bring finances to your attention. Be alert; analyze patterns and habits. Seek bargains for goods and services. The December 21 Yuletide eclipse in Gemini profoundly affects partnerships. An old bond may be dissolving and a new one forming. Others surprise you. The winter days are brightened January 8–February 4 by Venus in Sagittarius. A happy time for love develops. During February and March first Jupiter, then Uranus will change signs, to cross your 5th house cusp. This brings relief from ongoing family and housing concerns. Late winter promises an enjoyable romance or avocation. On March 2 Venus enters your 3rd house where it joins Neptune. Short journeys, upbeat conversations, and improved relationships with neighbors and siblings highlight winter's final weeks. Write a poem or short story.

HEALTH
Stubborn Taurus sits in your health sector. The positive side of this is that through sheer determination you often can rise above health challenges. The downside is that overindulgence and bad habits can be hard to break. While Venus is retrograde in your 12th house October 9–November 18, resolve to make needed changes. With Jupiter, your ruler, moving into a fire sign on January 23, the end of the year favors healing.

LOVE
Prepare for an exceptional year for romance. Uranus, the planet of sparkles and surprises, is about to enter your sector of love for a 7-year stay. It teases the cusp May 28–August 13, then reenters for the long haul on March 12. The eclipse at the winter solstice on December 21 is a Full Moon in Gemini, your 7th house of partnership and commitment. An existing bond is going through some changes and will either dissolve so that a new love can enter or will deepen and grow in a new direction. Flexibility on your part will aid the love process and help you to bring it to a happy conclusion.

SPIRITUALITY
Your 9th house of spirituality is linked to Sun-ruled Leo. Sunrises and sunsets can mark spiritual breakthroughs. Take time to appreciate them; poetry and artwork glorifying sunrises and sunsets can uplift you. The seasonal changes at the solstices and equinoxes are deeply spiritual times for you. The Elk is your shamanic animal guide. This magnificent animal wanders over vast distances and is considered quite territorial.

FINANCE
During the past couple of years Pluto has begun a very long passage through your 2nd house of finances. The changes in the world's financial structure have impacted your security. Saturn is leaving your 10th house of worldly fame and fortune, where it has formed a challenging square to your Sun. The financial picture brightens. A hint of this comes March 21–April 7 when Saturn touches the cusp. There will be some old matters to address until July 21, when the better cycle begins with aplomb.

CAPRICORN

The year ahead for those
born under the sign of the Goat
December 22–January 19

Lo! The things of nature, various,
One by one have left our sight;
Such are we, in life precarious,
Solstice Sun turns, to seek the light.

Goal-oriented and serious, you tend to respect traditions and rules. A stellar reputation is always a consideration. Natural aptitudes in math, music, building, finance, and farming characterize you. The knees, skin, teeth, and skeletal structure have a traditional link to Capricorn and can be at the root of health concerns.

Early spring finds Saturn, your ruler, in retrograde motion. It's a wonderful cycle to draw upon experience as a source of guidance. Past life recollections can develop. Through April 7 a cardinal T-square aspect involving Saturn, Pluto, and several Aries transits dynamically impacts you. You'll want to take action and focus on the "now." The New Moon in Aries on April 14 puts the focus on home life. Welcome the new season with a spring cleaning and a sage smudge.

Mercury remains in your love sector from early April until June 10. Communication and travel can impact romance. There might be multiple admirers. On June 8 Mars joins Saturn in Virgo to trine your Sun. This is a powerful, favorable combination impacting your 9th house. Your workload is easier to cope with and you'll have tremendous energy. Travel, study, writing projects, and the interests of in-laws, grandparents, and grandchildren all take a turn for the better through the end of July. The lunar eclipse at the Full Moon on June 26 conjoins Pluto in your sign, ushering in an intense time of self discovery. Throughout the rest of the year hidden talents surface; it's a time of surprises, growth, and change. A solar eclipse on July 11 in your 7th house can emphasize a legal matter or obligations to a partner. Compromise contributes to progress.

From Lammastide through August 6 Venus is favorable. Vacation travel is enjoyable. Share foreign cuisine or imported items with a loved one. During the remainder of August several transits in your 10th house bring deep involvement in career challenges. Patience and extra effort earn you respect and success as the summer ends. The New Moon on September 8 in Virgo conjoins Mercury. A four-week cycle of heightened mental activity commences. You'll understand confusing issues and make wise choices.

During most of October Venus and Mars travel through your 11th house. A deeper sense of community develops. November 8–29 Venus stations and turns direct in your career sector. Job politics are important. Consideration and friendliness at work can open windows of opportunity and make your responsibilities more enjoyable. In early December both Mercury and Mars enter your sign. Expect a hectic and active holiday season. Focus and concentrate. By your birthday future plans are full of promise.

On January 4 a solar eclipse in Capricorn conjoins both Mars and Pluto. Security issues are in a state of flux. There is an intensity present, affecting key issues such as family life, health, and career. January 14–February 3 finds Mercury moving rapidly over your Sun, making it easier to think through and resolve problems. Venus brightens your life February 5–March 1. Both love and financial prospects improve. Splurge on new garments, try a different hair style, or relax with a spa treatment. Others will notice and respond favorably. Be alert to extra income potential.

The first week of March Mercury joins Uranus in your 3rd house. Stay informed about current events, including world news and the latest trends in your field. The New Moon on March 4 highlights the specifics. This is an excellent time to catch up on correspondence. On March 12 Uranus joins Jupiter in Aries, marking significant developments in your home and family sector. Winter ends with a residential move or domestic improvements being considered.

HEALTH

Mercury-ruled Gemini oversees your 6th house of health. There are three retrograde Mercury cycles in earth signs this year. All are favorable for you. This is a wonderful time to overcome any existing health conditions. Two eclipses in your sign indicate that this will be an important year with surprise situations to cope with. Your vitality can be affected by all of the excitement. Meet the challenge by taking good care of yourself.

LOVE

April 1–25 brings a happy Venus transit through your 5th house of romance. The July 11 eclipse in Cancer creates a stir in your partnership and commitment sector. Expect turning points in an important relationship during the summer. The eclipse brings a favorable Venus aspect which lasts through August 6. Allow loved ones the freedom to be themselves and all will be well. February promises a more settled cycle regarding romance. You'll feel more confident and secure.

SPIRITUALITY

Saturn is completing a two-year passage through your 9th house on July 22. Your spiritual beliefs have been challenged by security issues and upset the status quo. Seeking practical solutions to real life challenges has been at the core of your spiritual quest. The Snow Goose is your shamanic animal guide. Always flying in a distinctive V formation, this graceful bird is a keeper of tradition. It has the stamina to migrate vast distances. Its loyalty to its flock is legendary.

FINANCE

Neptune, the planet of illusion and confusion, is completing its final year in your 2nd house of finances. During the past decade you've experienced a complete revamping of what security values and financial planning mean. A strong Pluto influence is present, helping you to be at peace with new financial patterns which affect the masses. The Full Moon of July 25 directly affects your finances. It coincides with favorable earth sign transits and ushers in a cycle of opportunity and greater security.

AQUARIUS
The year ahead for those
born under the sign of the Water Bearer
January 20–February 18

All ye who move in luxury's glow,
On whom kind plenty heaps her store,
If you have a charitable heart
that feels for woe,
Take in the wanderers at your door.

Generous, inspiring, and progressive, you are always curious about the future. There is ability in technology and science as well as a fascination with metaphysics. Extremes of body temperature can be a challenge as Aquarius has a link to the circulatory system. Since the ankles are also ruled by your sign, do be mindful of them.

Spring arrives with a competitive mood brewing, due to a Mars opposition in force through the first week of June. Be diplomatic and good humored with ornery people. During April Venus blesses your home and family sector. It's a perfect time to improve or decorate your home and to entertain there. The first three weeks of May show favorable influences in your 5th house of love and romance. Arrange a short outing or share thoughts about an interesting book with someone you're attracted to.

Your 1st and 5th houses benefit May 21–June 21 when Mercury trines Neptune. Interesting travel, new creative pursuits, good times with children and loved ones all make the late spring an exceptionally happy cycle. Heed your intuition. After the summer solstice the June 26 eclipse accents your 12th house. You'll desire more quiet time for stress release and contemplation, yet feel an urge to help troubled people or animals. The Aquarius Full Moon on July 25 enables you to express your feelings more easily, and others feel comfortable about opening up to you.

August finds Mars and Saturn favorably placed in your 9th house. Spiritual and intellectual advancement comes easily all month. September 1–13 can bring confusion regarding investments or financial decisions made by another, for Mercury is retrograde in your 8th house. Gather facts and postpone action if in doubt. Just after Mabon Mercury moves toward an opposition with both Jupiter and your ruling planet, Uranus. Double-check claims and credentials. This isn't the best time for a financial risk. On the other hand the 8th house influence does favor contact with the spirit world. A séance or ghost hunt during the first days of autumn should be very successful.

During October a planetary stellium forms in your 10th house of career. Recognition from others and a deep sense of personal accomplishment come by Samhain. At Hallowmas ceremonies, bless your work space and offer thanks for your natural aptitudes. November 8–29 Venus and Saturn in your 9th house promise productive travel. It's a good time to network with a spouse's family and relatives of other age groups. Try foreign cuisine and learn conversational phrases in another language.

December 1–18 Mercury joins Pluto in your 12th house. Overcome worry and anxiety through faith. You can create your own heaven (or Hades) in the theater of your thoughts. The December 21 eclipse at Yuletide profoundly impacts your love sector. A great awakening concerning romance can occur. Bless some mistletoe. Leave it hanging in your dwelling to create goodwill during the entire year ahead. Act upon breakthrough creative ideas you have at this Full Moon.

January begins with a strong 11th house influence. Friends reach out to you; plans are discussed. January 16–February 22 Mars transits your sign and conjoins other Aquarius planets. This is an extremely dynamic influence. Motivation and enthusiasm characterize this birthday. Control anger and impatience though. Affirm your personal focus and direction at the Candlemas New Moon on February 2. March dovetails in brightly with a Venus conjunction. Late winter holds the promise of great happiness regarding both finances and social life. Uranus, your ruler, changes signs on March 12. A pivotal conversation or short journey have the ability to open up new horizons.

HEALTH
The July 11 eclipse impacts your 6th house of health. During the summer heed subtle signals your body offers. Maintain a wholesome home environment. Family health history can provide valuable guidance. Uranus, your ruler, is making a rare sign change this year, touching the cusp of your 3rd house. Information comes your way during the weeks of May 28 and March 12 to offer insight concerning future guidelines toward the condition of wellness.

LOVE
You often want a relationship, yet desire much independence. Retrograde Mercury cycles can bring back a lost love. They also usher in repeating patterns related to affairs of the heart, for better or worse. Postpone either making or breaking commitments while Mercury is retrograde. The December eclipse in Gemini brings great shifts regarding love. Cultivate important relationships in May, August, and March when Venus smiles on your opportunities.

SPIRITUALITY
Mystical Neptune is completing the final year of a long passage through Aquarius. You are deciding which spiritual practices are meaningful and which to leave behind. Saturn crosses the cusp of Libra, ruler of your 9th house of philosophy and spirituality, in July. You'll seek teachings which address real life issues. Your shamanic animal guide is the Otter. Whimsical, playful, and curious, Otter brings the wisdom of humor and receptivity to other creatures.

FINANCE
For the last seven years Uranus has brought volatility to your 2nd house of money. A more settled trend develops when Uranus begins its sign change in late May. Benevolent Jupiter conjoins Uranus and brings some wonderful financial prospects from the vernal equinox through June 6 and again September 10–January 22. Don't procrastinate. Pursue the opportunities which should be present during these periods.

PISCES

The year ahead for those
born under the sign of the Fish
February 19–March 20

Ice bound are streams
which strive to flow,
Through groves where the
warblers, birds, have sung;
And fields are shrouded deep in snow,
Yet soon bright violets will have sprung.

Imaginative, empathetic, visionary, and sensitive, you are vulnerable to your surroundings. Often charitable, Pisceans are natural artists or healers. Physically, the feet are related to this sign. The health of the whole body can be impacted by the strength and comfort of your feet and toes.

Spring's earliest days find Jupiter midway through your birth sign. Enjoy a cycle of great growth and opportunity which accelerates until early June. March 21–31 Venus brightens your financial sector. An aptitude can generate extra income by All Fool's Day. Mars creates a stir in your 6th house, which relates to animal companions. Be careful about adopting a new pet during April. Make sure it's in harmony with your household first.

During May a favorable Mercury influence enables you to overcome any mental blocks generated either by traumatic learning experiences or frustration. A once elusive subject is suddenly an open book. The New Moon on May 13 marks a turning point after which ideas flow more freely. From May 20 through mid-June Venus dances through Cancer, ruler of your 5th house of love. A romance is very promising. At the same time, however, a Mars opposition agitates June 8–July 29. Partnerships and other relationships require patience. The eclipse of July 11 again impacts your sector of love and romance. A change of heart can occur quite suddenly. On the positive side, creative abilities and relationships with children can take a turn for the better. You'll understand where your affections truly lie and act accordingly.

At Lammas a strong 8th house influence begins to develop. You'll embark on some detective work or a research project. A series of synchronicities reinforces your faith in the afterlife. On August 24 the Full Moon in Pisces heightens your intuition and offers inspiration. Venus begins a long passage through Scorpio on September 9. Travel, spiritual activities, and higher education are sources of great joy through early January. Studies related to the fine arts can be especially rewarding. Love assumes an elevated and ethereal tone by Mabon.

Late October–November 8 Mercury and the Sun combine in a favorable trine aspect to your sign. Valuable ideas come your way near Samhain. Gather information. During November both of your ruling planets, Jupiter and Neptune, complete retrograde cycles. You find ways to satisfactorily conclude old business in order to step forward. With Mars in your career sector, you feel more motivated regarding professional aspirations.

By December 8 Mercury, Pluto, and Mars move together in Capricorn, your 11th house. Goals and humanitarian projects are important. The eclipse on December 21 emphasizes home and family needs. Changes in the life of a relative can affect your own plans. Rise to the occasion and all will be well. The solar eclipse on January 4 brings another shift in focus. January 8–February 4 Venus favorably aspects Neptune, your ruler. The 10th house is involved. Opportunities develop which permit you to express your natural gifts and heart's desire at work. Influential people are impressed. At Candlemas purchase a small mirror, meditate on your own reflection by dim light, and visualize yourself surrounded by all that you admire and desire.

As your birthday nears, Mercury moves rapidly in conjunction with the Sun. The pace of daily life picks up; pursue travel opportunities. Your eloquent writing and speaking skills open doors. Your confidence attracts others to you near the New Moon in Pisces on March 4. The winter concludes with Mars in your sign. You're motivated and anxious to move forward. Use reasonable caution regarding athletic events, winter sports, or other physically demanding activities.

HEALTH
The Sun has a special link to your well-being. Spend a few minutes each day outdoors in the full spectrum light. During the winter turn on extra lights to revive energy. An aromatherapy lamp can be very effective. Try peppermint oil to relieve overall aches and pains, basil for low energy, lavender to lift depression, or lemon for cleansing and clearing.

LOVE
Loved ones might have personal issues to resolve due to a Saturn opposition involving your 7th house of partnerships April 8–July 20. Is a situation too broken to be fixed? The July 11 eclipse in your romance sector ushers in startling new developments this year. Venus transits during late May–mid-June and December are harmonious. Since Cancer rules romance in your horoscope, a loved one's home and family heritage can reveal compatibility potentials. Near the January 19 Full Moon in Cancer, serve a favorite childhood recipe to your sweetheart as a romantic dinner.

SPIRITUALITY
Inscrutable Pluto rules your spirituality. A dread of being misunderstood can pose a hurdle to your spiritual development. Explore spiritual expression using art and music while a long Venus transit from early September to early January impacts your 9th house. The Cougar is your animal guide. This graceful cat is so elusive and silent that Native Americans often thought it was a spirit, not a real creature at all.

FINANCE
Jupiter and Uranus both enter your financial sector this year, pointing to favorable expansion and fresh sources of income. Look for a hint of the specifics in late May and early June. The winter season, after January 23, brings this promising influence to fruition. Pursue profits through grass-roots enterprises and your ideas for new ventures.

Sites of Awe

Jerusalem

Certain spots on the planet exert an old, old magic. Such places open our hearts, take us out of our ordinary lives and into fresh realms. This year chance provided our up close and personal traveler with an amazing journey to Jerusalem and visits to supremely holy sites.

The Church of the Holy Sepulcher

I had a feeling of pilgrimage treading the narrow twisting streets of the Old City that wind to the holiest site of Christianity. Here at the end of narrow streets arises the Church of the Holy Sepulcher, a structure covering sites of both the Crucifixion and the tomb of Christ. Along the way I see people walking the Stations of the Cross, the Via Dolorosa. The sacred path is marked in the ancient Jerusalem stone walls, each marking regarded as another step. The markers are regarded with tearful emotion by the devotees, many of whom pause and venerate each one. The Church has had a tumultuous history. Built in the fourth century by Constantine, the first Christian Emperor,

the structure had been destroyed and rebuilt a grievous number of times until the Crusaders carried out a huge restoration in the twelfth century. Down the years the structure has seen frequent rebuilding and what we see today is mainly from an 1810 remodeling.

Various groups control parts of the building and hold regular services, including the Greek, Roman, Armenian and Coptic churches. The interior reflects a confusion of architectural styles reflecting the numerous eras and interests. Near the entrance is the Stone of Anointing, where the body of Jesus was sanctified with spices before burial according to Jewish custom. Upstairs is the Greek Orthodox Calvary, the site where Christ was crucified and covering the actual Rock of Golgotha. These are places to be experienced, absolutely beyond any words of description.

The Western Wall

I visited the sacred structure with the intention of praying for world peace, a prayer I felt was probably shared by many of the swaying figures around me. It is customary to write one's prayer on a little note and poke it between the yellow-white stones. But the time is both Chanukah and Shebat, the Sabbath, and I knew that no writing nor virtually any activity takes place on the day devoted solely to God. In my pocket I find an olive leaf I had picked up in the Old City that morning. I seem to have sacramental feelings about olive trees, so I breathe my prayer into the leaf and insert it into a crack.

The site, also known as the "Wailing Wall," is especially crowded for the occasion. I am engulfed in the drone of Hebrew prayers, sometimes interspersed by single invocations or Torah readings. The feeling of prayers flowing over my head and body is overwhelming as I imagine the countless numbers of people who have journeyed here to pray. A screen separates men and women to avoid distractions, according to Orthodox practice. Most stand, others sit on plastic chairs. Many men wear tallises, elaborate prayer shawls, and all wear hats or *yarmulkes*, the skullcaps available in boxes nearby. Women are required to wear shawls and cover-ups for short skirts, also provided.

The vicinity is the most sacred site in Jewish observance. The plaza area surrounds the remains of the Temple of Solomon, built above the Temple Mount in the second century B.C.E. Solomon's glorious architecture was destroyed by the Romans in 70 C.E., eternal occasion for grief. But the remains extend deep into the earth and attest to the rabbinic faith that the Divine Presence never departs from the Temple Mount, the Judaic "Holy of Holies."

Mount Moriah (Hebrew: Har haBáyit), also known as The Temple Mount and by Muslims as the Noble Sanctuary *(Arabic: al haram al qudsi ash sharif)*. Mount Moriah within the Western Wall also has profound significance for Muslims. They believe that angels visited the Rock two thousand years before Adam, and that the site is surrounded daily by seventy thousand angels. Islamic traditions also hold that at this location Mohammed ascended to heaven on his steed, El Buraq. And here, Muslims believe, Israfil will blow the last trumpet on Resurrection Day, when the dead rise from their graves. There is a feeling of loftiness as I stand in the century-old marketplace and stare up at the mighty gold dome. I can sense the "might of heaven" as I look upon the gold dome with a backdrop of the blue sky.

The gleaming Dome of the Rock is visible throughout the city and I am eager to be admitted inside this sacred Muslim site, but it is available to visitors only in peaceful times. Perhaps those will be prevailing on my next visit...

– ARMAND TABER

Sites of Awe photos can be found on wwwTheWitchesAlmanac.com/sites-of-awe.html.

Wailing Wall, Jerusalem

Reviews

 The Moors
CDBABY http://
cdbaby.com/cd/themoors

Podcast/Website:
A Darker Shade of Pagan
http://www.adarkershadeofpagan.com/

IF YOU BUY one CD this year, buy "The Moors." This magnificent work has been around for many years and has been released many times under many labels, but what is important is that it is available again now from cdbaby.com. Quoting their website [http://www.mobiusbandwidth.com/themoors.html] "The music of the Moors (guitarist/electronic whiz Scott Dakota, and singer/flautist Sharynne nic Macha) transcends genre, blending gothic, ambient, rock, ethereal, Celtic traditional and tribal elements. The band describes their particular style as 'goth pagan trance rock,' but perhaps categorizing such a complex and engaging sound is not only difficult, but pointless."

I really can't say it better than that because it is just the plain truth of the matter. This is not a comfortable excursion into the realm of Fluffy Bunny neighborhood Neo-Paganism. This is a sound excursion designed to inflame your passions and awaken the ancient memories buried within.

Go there now. Your ancestral ghosts are waiting for you.

IF MUSIC soothes the savage beast within you and informs your soul as it does mine, then you must open a web browser and point it at the URL for Jason Pitzl Walters Podcast site "A darker Shade of Pagan." This is an ongoing weekly podcast and streaming Internet radio show that looks at modern music from a unique spiritual perspective. The pagan perspective.

You do not need to own an iPod to enjoy the experience; you can play his weekly show directly from your browser. And if you do own an iPod, you can subscribe to the podcast and automatically download each week's offering.

The world of analog radio would never countenance a truly pagan show of this caliber. But we are twenty-first century witches and pagans, and Jason has earned a role as the Grand Summoner of our musical fate. Let him take you by the hand and journey into sonic landscapes that will open new worlds for you to explore. A Darker Shade of Pagan has opened me to a rich vein of new artists, and I believe that it will do so for you too.

Celtic Folk Soul: Art, Myth & Symbol by Jen Delyth, Amber Lotus Publishing, [http://www.celticfolksoul.com/]

DELYTH'S Celtic Folk Soul is a magnificently illustrated journey through the rich cultural heritage of the Celtic people. Jen Delyth is one of the best and most prolific Celtic artists of her generation and with this book she displays equal artistry at weaving her imagery with masterful storytelling. This book is an essential tool for those who enjoy imaginal sojourns in the landscapes of our Celtic Ancestors. Jen's has already made her mark in the Celtic genre with her "Celtic Tree Of Life" design [http://www.kelticdesigns.com] which is now iconic as a modern Celtic Folk motif. Once again Jen stands out from the pack and brings added dimension to the field with a work of stunning beauty and peerless style.

– OWEN ROWLEY

TO: The Witches' Almanac, P.O. Box 1292, Newport, RI 02840-9998
www.TheWitchesAlmanac.com

Name_____

Address_____

City_____ State_____ Zip_____

E-mail_____

WITCHCRAFT being by nature one of the secretive arts, it may not be as easy to find us next year. If you'd like to make sure we know where you are, why don't you send us your name and address? You will certainly hear from us.

From a Witch's Mailbox

communication as much as possible. Readers can help also – please check out "Green and Going Greener" on our website. As good stewards of the earth, we do whatever we can to reduce our carbon footprint.

Sites of Awe cited

We enjoy travel and especially liked your account in the last issue of the Horse of Uffington. We especially like traveling in England because it is easy to get around with no language problems. But this year we are on a tighter budget and will vacation in the U.S. Do you have any sites of awe kind of suggestions?

– Edwin Stafford
Brooklyn, N.Y.

Sure. Our trusty traveler Armand Taber has a great agenda lined up. In future issues he will be exploring at least one of the following awe-inspiring sites on American venues: the unique red rock setting of Sedona, Arizona, the dizzying, foamy magic of Niagara Falls and the giants of Sequoia Park, California.

Going green

I like the "green" project you mentioned on your website. When are you going to convert to recycled paper?

– Dorothy T.
e-mail

Thank you, Dorothy, we like readers on green alert. The answer to your question is "yesterday. " The issue you are reading is on pages of recycled paper. Our Green Campaign goes beyond saving paper and our staff uses digital

Ask the Sky Maiden

I love the astrology section of the Almanac, but I always have more questions. For instance, why don't you show the retrogrades of the outer planets?

– Maria Gonzales
Miami, Florida

Not in the realm of the possible. Our staff astrologer, Dikki-Jo Mullen, points out that these planets do not create a significant enough change in the course of a year to identify with a broad group of twelve Sun signs. If you'd like to know how the outer planet retrogrades and other transits affect you on a personal level, you can purchase a personal horoscope from Dikki-Jo. See her ad on page 143 for details

Amazed bull

I am young and don't have too many books yet. Can you tell me where I can find some stuff on the Greek bull called Minotaur I saw once in a cartoon?

– Arthur Bartoni
Detroit. Michigan

In an ideal world schools would be teaching the Greek myths, exciting stories that have come down to us in many forms over thousands of years. The Minotaur was half human, half white bull. In Crete he was imprisoned by a king in a maze that no one could penetrate. Every year young people had to be sacrificed to the Minotaur until the hero Theseus discovered how to slay the bull and find his way out. If you want to learn more, check out our *Greek Gods in Love* by Barbara Stacy, an enjoyable introductory version of the stories with great illustrations.

New products, your ideas?

Will the Almanac have any new products available on your website in the near future? I already have one each of all your bracelets and use the various gems for purposes as noted.

– Beatrice S.
e-mail

We are happy that you are enjoying the bracelets. Yes, we are in the course of planning more products to feature on the website. If you or any of our readers would like to suggest new Almanac wares, we would welcome any ideas sent to our e-mail address below.

Learning spells

What is a good way to learn spells?

– Deidre Merliss
e-mail

Judika Illes is a terrific source of information about charms. She is the author of the authoritative The Element Encyclopedia of 5,000 Charms. *According to Judika, "My spiritual vision incorporates the application of Earth's ancient magical and therapeutic traditions for the fulfillment of modern needs and desires. "You can learn a spell today just by accessing our Almanac website – every week we post a new charm from Judika.*

Walk the walk

Several years ago you ran an article on the labyrinth. Can you tell me what issue that was from?

– Mary Beth Lucas
e-mail

That was "The Labyrinth" from the 2001/2002 issue, and it offered classic patterns that were simply winding paths – no trickery or confusion intended. They were created for purposes of walking meditation. Walking the path inspires focus, clears the mind, and may give insight into the spiritual journey. Once you started, if you kept on keeping on, you would arrive at the center and simply retrace your way out.

Let us hear from you, too

We love to hear from our readers. Letters should be sent with the writer's name (or just first name or initials), address, daytime phone number and e-mail address, if available. Published material may be edited for clarity or length. All letters and e-mails will become the property of The Witches' Almanac Ltd. and will not be returned. We regret that due to the volume of correspondence we cannot reply to all communications.

The Witches' Almanac, Ltd.
P.O. Box 1292
Newport, RI 02840-9998
info@TheWitchesAlmanac.com
www.TheWitchesAlmanac.com

News from The Witches' Almanac

Glad tidings from the staff

Three new editions

The Horned Shepherd by Edgar Jepson. The Wise Ones recognize an ancient fertility god who should be sacrificed to enrich the land. The new Witches' Almanac version of the fantasy novella, written in 1904, features beautiful woodcuts by Wilfred Jones. $16.95

The ABC of Magic Charms. A treasury of amulets, talismans, charms and fetishes – symbols of the mystical from prehistoric times to the present. An enlarged version of a perennial favorite edition. $12.95

The Little Book of Magical Creatures by Elizabeth Pepper and Barbara Stacy. Our kin in the animal kingdom – creatures tame, wild and fabulous. Reissue and expansion of an earlier Creatures publication, with a new section of myths from other places, other times. A must for animal lovers. $12.95

Going Green

In our ongoing effort to help Mother Earth, this year *The Witches' Almanac* is printed on recycled paper! Remember to do your part by signing up for our email newsletter on our website at http://TheWitchesAlmanac.com/emailform.html.

Great website browsing, www.TheWitchesAlmanac.com

Almanac Extras. Sometimes we get excited by material for which we have too limited page space – sometimes a whole article, sometimes addenda of a printed piece. These become the Extras, of which at this writing nine are offered. Informative, entertaining reading, updated from time to time. See these Extras at our website www.TheWitchesAlmanac.com.

- *Weekly spells*. From spell authority Judika Illes
- *Sites of Awe photos*. Accompaniments to Armand Taber's journeys to significant places.
- *Mentors*. Many of us are experiencing trying economic times and feeling disoriented. A new web link features suggestions both mystical and practical.

New calendar year for Horoscopes

In addition to beginning our astrological calendar year in March with Aries as usual, the Almanac will retain the three previous signs of Capricorn, Aquarius and Pisces. Often appreciated at the winter holiday season, now the horoscopes can be enjoyed without a three-month wait.

YouTube

The Witches' Almanac is proud to be represented on YouTube by Chloe, an Almanac staff member with a passion for cooking. In this video, Chloe shares her treasured recipe for Rosemary Shortbread, always a hit at our holiday parties. Go to www.YouTube.com and search *"The Witches' Almanac"*.

New Distributor

The Witches' Almanac is now distributed by Red Wheel/Weiser/Conari – a new incarnation of the time honored Samuel Weiser of New York City.

Almanac lack?

For your convenience, if a shop in your area doesn't carry the Almanac or its publications, please let us know and we will contact them. Thank you for the heads up!

Personalized Specialty Horoscopes Created Just For You!

by Dikki-Jo Mullen,
The Witches' Almanac Astrologer

Crystal Wheel Horoscopes

Send your month, day, year, time and place of birth and Dikki-Jo will create a beautiful wooden horoscope plaque with crystals, shells and sharks teeth symbolizing your own astrological placements. Approx. 8" by 10", ready to hang. Hand crafted original. Includes interpretation. Astrological symbols and birth stones traditionally are linked to great good luck. $125.00 (post paid)

Floral Horoscopes

Send your birth data and Dikki-Jo will create an original painting using pastels and acrylics of the flowers linked to your Sun, Moon and Ascendant. Approx. 12" x 10", ready to display. Interpretation included, your astrological flowers traditionally relate to growth, healing and good luck. $125.00 (post paid)

Order by check or money order and mail to:

Dikki-Jo Mullen, PO Box 533024, Orlando, Florida 32853
407-895-1522 or 321-773-1414

Please allow about three weeks for delivery by Priority Mail.

**Convention Programs, Personal Readings,
Complete Astrology Consultation Services,
Classes, Group Presentations Available**

⚬ CLASSIFIEDS ⚬

Greek Gods in Love
Barbara Stacy

*New versions of timeless love tales –
lively, witty, entertaining*

The author casts a marvelously original eye on the beloved stories of Greek deities, replete with amorous oddities and escapades. The glittering mythology resonates with Eros, love in all its astounding variety – devotional, perfidious, sunny, dark, frenzied, serene, lusty, uncanny, earthy, twisty, and sometimes hilarious. We relish these tales in all their splendor and antic humor, and offer an inspired storyteller's fresh version of the old, old mythical magic.

Lavishly illustrated with 190 designs drawn from ancient Greek art. Visual delights abound. $15.95 Paperback, 120 pages, 9" x 11"

Available from Olympian Press…

Good Luck Bracelets

Gemstones are cherished by the wise for their life-enhancing values. The right gems help bring you luck. These matched gems on stretchable one-size-fits-all cords make beautiful accessories. Wear one or more, as long as their purposes do not conflict.

Bracelets are packed in pouches with legends about their properties. Visit our website at www.TheWitchesAlmanac.com to view the bracelets and read their legends. $5.95 each, $2.00 shipping/handling. Wholesale inquiries welcome.

The Witches' Almanac Book Bag

Tasteful Toting

Complimentary with any purchase over $100, or $17.95 each, $4.00 shipping/handling.

The Witches' Almanac logo and the medieval woodcut design take you through the day in mystic style.

The tasteful canvas bag, measuring 17" x 13" x 5," with a 20" strap, carries whatever you fancy – books, clothes, laptop, cardcase, lunch, water, makeup, secrets, it's your space.

Choice of black on natural or black on red. Wholesale inquiries welcome.

front

back

And a special offer – Count on your own free book bag if you order an Almanac Bundle, 13 back issues, $75 (a $117.00 value). 1993/4 through the 2005/6 Almanac.

Our books available by mail order:

A Treasury from past editions…

Witches All

Perfect for study or casual reading, Witches All *is a collection from* The Witches' Almanac *publications of the past. Arranged by topics, the book, like the popular almanacs, is thought provoking and often spurs me on to a tangent leading to even greater discovery.*

The information and art in the book—astrological attributes, spells, recipes, history, facts & figures is a great reminder of the history of the Craft, not just in recent years, but in the early days of the Witchcraft Revival in this century: the witch in an historical and cultural perspective.

Ty Bevington, Circle of the Wicker Man,
Columbus, Ohio

Absolutely beautiful! I recently ordered Witches All *and I have to say I wasn't disappointed. The artwork and articles are first rate and for a longtime* Witches' Almanac *fan, it is a wonderful addition to my collection.* Witches' Almanac *devotees and newbies alike will love this latest effort. Very worth getting.*

Tarot3, Willits, California

MAGIC CHARMS FROM A TO Z

A treasury of amulets, talismans, fetishes and other lucky objects compiled by the staff of *The Witches' Almanac.* An invaluable guide for all who respond to the call of mystery and enchantment.

LOVE CHARMS

Love has many forms, many aspects. Ceremonies performed in witchcraft celebrate the joy and the blessings of love. Here is a collection of love charms to use now and ever after.

MAGICAL CREATURES

Mystic tradition grants pride of place to many members of the animal kingdom. Some share our life. Others live wild and free. Still others never lived at all, springing instead from the remarkable power of human imagination.

ANCIENT ROMAN HOLIDAYS

The glory that was Rome awaits you in Barbara Stacy's classic presentation of a festive year in pagan times. Here are the gods and goddesses as the Romans conceived them, accompanied by the annual rites performed in their worship. Scholarly, light-hearted – a rare combination.

CELTIC TREE MAGIC

Robert Graves in *The White Goddess* writes of the significance of trees in the old Celtic lore. *Celtic Tree Magic* is an investigation of the sacred trees in the remarkable Beth-Luis-Nion alphabet; their role in folklore, poetry, and mysticism.

MOON LORE

As both the largest and the brightest object in the night sky, and the only one to appear in phases, the Moon has been a rich source of myth for as long as there have been mythmakers.

MAGIC SPELLS AND INCANTATIONS

Words have magic power. Their sound, spoken or sung, has ever been a part of mystic ritual. From ancient Egypt to the present, those who practice the art of enchantment have drawn inspiration from a treasury of thoughts and themes passed down through the ages.

LOVE FEASTS

Creating meals to share with the one you love can be a sacred ceremony in itself. With the witch in mind, culinary adept Christine Fox offers magical menus and recipes for every month in the year.

RANDOM RECOLLECTIONS I, II, III, IV

Pages culled from the original (no longer available) issues of *The Witches' Almanac,* published annually throughout the 1970's, are now available in a series of tasteful booklets. A treasure for those who missed us the first time around; keepsakes for those who remember.

Order form on back page

Order Form

Special offer – *1993/94 Almanac through the 2005/06 Almanac*
Bundle of 13 back issues for only $75, with free book bag. (*$117.00 value*)

The Witches' Almanac

___ 2010-2011, ___2009-2010 @ $11.95 _____
___2008-2009 @ $10.95 _____
___2007-2008 @ $9.95 _____
___ 2006-2007, ___ 2005-2006, ___ 2004-2005, ___ 2003-2004 @ $8.95 _____
___ 2002-2003, ___ 2001-2002, ___ 2000-2001, ___ 1999-2000 @ $7.95 _____
___ 1998-1999, ___ 1997-1998, ___ 1996-1997, ___ 1995-1996 @ $6.95 _____
___ 1994-1995, ___ 1993-1994 @ $5.95 _____
___ Bundle of 13 back issues (*Free book bag*) @ $75.00 _____
___ Witches All @ $13.95 _____
Random Recollections (*volume* I *sold out*) ___ II, ___ III, ___ IV @ $3.95 _____

Bracelets and Book Bags

___ Agate, Green	___ Agate, Moss	___ Agate, Natural	___ Agate, Red
___ Amethyst	___ Aventurine	___ Fluorite	___ Jade, African
___ Jade, White	___ Jasper, Picture	___ Jasper, Red	___ Lapis Lazuli
___ Malachite	___ Moonstone	___ Obsidian	___ Onyx, Black
___ Opal	___ Quartz Crystal	___ Quartz, Rose	___ Rhodonite
___ Sodalite	___ Tigereye	___ Turquoise	___ Unakite

Total Number of Bracelets x $5.95 _____

___ Natural/Black Book Bag   ___ Red/Black Book Bag
Total Number of Book Bags x $17.95 _____

Other Publications

___ The Horned Shepherd @ $16.95 _____
___ Greek Gods In Love @ $15.95 _____
(*original*)___ Magic Charms from A to Z @ $12.95 _____
(*expanded*)___ The ABC of Magic Charms @ $12.95 _____
___ Love Charms @ $6.95 _____
(*original*)___ Magical Creatures @ $12.95 _____
(*expanded*)___ The Little Book of Magical Creatures @ $12.95 _____
___ Ancient Roman Holidays @ $6.95 _____
___ Celtic Tree Magic @ $7.95 _____
___ Moon Lore @ $7.95 _____
___ Magic Spells and Incantations @ $12.95 _____
___ Love Feasts @ $6.95 _____

Subtotal _____
Shipping & handling _____
(*One book: $4.00 Each additional book add $1.50; $2.00 per bracelet; $4.00 per book bag*)
Total _____

Send a check or money order payable in U. S. funds or credit card details to:
The Witches' Almanac, Ltd., PO Box 1292, Newport, RI 02840-9998
(401) 847-3388 (phone) • (888) 897-3388 (fax)
Email: info@TheWitchesAlmanac.com • www.TheWitchesAlmanac.com